GUERRILLA
WARFARE
WEAPONS

GUERRILLA WARFARE WEAPONS

The modern underground
fighter's armoury

TERRY GANDER

Sterling Publishing Co., Inc.   New York

Cover illustration by Robert Partridge

10   9   8   7   6   5   4   3   2   1

Published in 1990 by Sterling Publishing Co., Inc.
387 Park Avenue South, New York, N.Y. 10016
Published in Great Britain by Patrick Stephens Ltd,
part of the Thorsens Publishing Group. © 1989 by Terry Gander
Distributed in Canada by Sterling Publishing
% Canadian Manda Group, P.O. Box 920, Station U
Toronto, Ontario, Canada M8Z 5P9
Manufactured in the United States of America
Sterling ISBN 0-8069-7333-1 Paper

CONTENTS

AN INTRODUCTION TO THE GUERRILLA

If it were possible to do nothing other than read through a selection of all the newspapers published since 1945, the conclusion might soon be reached that the guerrilla is a phenomenon of modern times. The years since 1945 bear witness to an unremitting onslaught from a wide selection of people, who have carried out lethal activities under a variety of banners. They have ranged from political activists aiming for declared limited objectives, to freedom fighters, liberation activists, revolutionaries, and downright thugs, and their activities have ranged from those of woolly-minded social stirrers, who produce little other than nuisance value behaviour, to those of trained and determined terrorists, who are a danger to any established regime or way of life.

Whatever label such people care to adopt, they nearly all come under the blanket designation of guerrilla. The guerrilla in his (or her) many forms has become such an established figure on the world stage over the last few decades that it has become a commonplace assumption that the guerrilla is a purely modern phenomenon. Nothing could be further from the truth: the guerrilla has played a part in social unrest since before historical records were kept. Many of the early recorded conflicts, such as those mentioned in the Old Testament, can be regarded as little other than guerrilla campaigns, often carried out by both sides involved. Many long-established conflicts have never advanced beyond anything other than low-key warfare, little removed from what we now define as guerrilla activity; the history of the last few centuries is dotted with instances of guerrilla warfare of all kinds. What may be regarded as the culmination of guerrilla warfare as an established practice took place when the Communist Chinese won power from the previous Chinese governing bodies in 1949. That takeover followed a guerrilla conflict that can be traced back over two decades, involving campaigns against both the Chinese Kuomintang and the Japanese occupation forces.

The Communist Chinese victory seemed to mark the point where what had formerly been an unplanned and extemporized method of fighting became an established form of modern warfare, but it was in reality only a marker on the page of history. There was nothing the Communists carried out on their way to becoming a new order that had not been employed as standard practice by unknown numbers of guerrillas in other combat scenarios fought out over the years. But be that as it may, the guerrilla is now almost an accepted part of modern life; yet a study of history will soon demonstrate that the guerrilla has been around for a very long time.

What then is a guerrilla? One dictionary definition of the guerrilla is 'a member of an irregular, usually politically-motivated armed force that combats stronger regular forces, such as the army or police.' The word 'guerrilla' is derived from the diminutive of the Spanish *guerra* and thus denotes 'little war', which seems to sum up what we now define as guerrilla warfare quite nicely. The term dates from the period of the French occupation of Spain, which lasted from 1807 to 1813 – the Spanish word for a fighter in the warfare that then ensued is *guerrillero*. Modern terms for guerrilla warfare vary widely, from 'low-intensity warfare' to 'counter-insurgency' or 'counter-terrorist warfare', all being terms used usually by the regular forces involved. The guerrilla likes to use terms such as 'revolutionary warfare', 'freedom struggle', 'liberation movement', and so on.

The dictionary definition can be taken as a neat summation of the guerrilla and his method of combat. The guerrilla is nearly always someone who has decided to desert their normal mode of life and undertake some form of improvised military operation against an established power, that might be either internal or external in origin. This does not rule out the involvement of trained military personnel in guerrilla operations. Throughout history, guerrilla groups have been led by, or have involved, trained regular military personnel of all ranks and stages of expertise – Tito's partisans in wartime Yugoslavia being a case in point. But whatever their origins, the guerrilla is one who undertakes a definite course of action that involves combat against an established power or force, and undertakes that course of action in whatever manner possible.

Over the years, guerrilla groupings have been involved in so many operations in so many areas of the world and against so many regimes that it is impossible to provide a precise definition of the guerrilla that applies in all situations. Some guerrilla movements have come to an abrupt end in bloodshed and misery. Others have degenerated from high ideals to banditry and plunder. Many groups have disintegrated through internal squabbling – radical political movements seem prone to internal schism and perpetual argument over ideals and details of policy. Yet others have achieved their original goals and have become established political forces, only to suffer the attentions of other guerrilla groupings seeking to undermine their authority.

The list of guerrilla activity is endless. Almost every nation now extant has suffered from the attentions of the guerrilla in some form or another, and some have never been free from their activities. The fortunate nations which, so far, have been relatively free from guerrilla activity, can only await their turn. It seems likely that the guerrilla phenomenon will come to all, in some form or another.

The disparity of guerrilla objectives is considerable. Some guerrillas fight for a concept such as freedom from occupation. Others fight for religious reasons, either to free their homeland from foreign religious interference, or perhaps the very opposite, to impose a particular brand of religious thought or behaviour on others. Perhaps the commonest and most widespread cause of modern times has been political, namely the infliction of a form of political order on others, who might otherwise be unwilling to assume such views: nearly all the guerrilla campaigns of the last 50 years have been motivated by political ideals, to a greater or lesser extent, with Marxism well to the fore. Nearly all Marxist-based movements have been successful, to some degree or other. Yet other motivation sources can easily be thought of. One example is the sheer love of power that leads individuals to form guerrilla bands and harry established regimes. More complex are the movements that arise to establish racial or ethnic homelands in the midst of larger populations. The Tamil separatists in Sri Lanka provide a prime example of the latter; an added dimension to the problem there (in Sri Lanka) is that Marxism has also intruded, to add a political spice to the ferment.

One aspect of modern guerrilla activity that can be readily distinguished is the division between urban guerrillas and rural guerrillas. While their motivations might well be the same, the two groupings operate along differing lines. Rural guerrillas can usually stay together for prolonged periods, and may operate in groups that vary in size from a mere handful to hundreds. Urban guerrillas, however, usually operate individually or in very small numbers, and then split up to carry on normal lives that are interrupted only when they again see fit to carry out their disruptive operations.

Guerrillas have one asset that their opposition usually lacks. They are highly mobile, and if the worst comes to the worst they can simply melt away in the surrounding population. Very few guerrillas wear uniforms or other forms of recognition, unless they are operating as arms of established regular armed forces - again, Tito's partisans provide an example. Even then, the partisans could frequently either melt away into the countryside or remove their uniforms and hide within the towns and cities. Very often, guerrillas can call upon passive support from the local populace, in the form of shelter, food, hiding places for weapons and supplies and the provision of rest areas. Such help might be paid for with labour, education, or promise of future rewards.

Passive (or active) support from the community is essential for successful guerrilla activity. Guerrillas attempting to operate in the midst of a hostile populace will soon be given away or, at best, will be denied assistance or other forms of support; this remains as true for the urban guerrilla as for their rural counterparts. Despite the uproar and disruption that groups such as the West German Baader-Meinhof Gang managed to produce in the mid-seventies, they were eventually hunted down and destroyed for the simple reason that they gained little support outside their immediate social circle. The 'oppressed masses' they wished to free wanted nothing to do with them. By contrast, other guerrilla groups as disparate as the IRA and the Afghan Mujahideen continue to prosper among populations where many are sympathetic or passively supportive to their causes.

Despite the great variety of guerrillas and guerrilla operations, it is possible to break down the sequence of their overall operational activities into four main stages. The first is the creation of a network in which the guerrilla can operate. This involves recruitment, personnel selection, the creation of weapon and supply depots, the training of personnel, and so on. At this stage the guerrilla organization is often under the close supervision of a highly-motivated individual who will, in time, emerge as the guerrillas' overall leader. Around him he will create a small and trusted group of cohorts who will act as his lieutenants, messengers and possible future deputies. The leader will probably have in mind a definite objective, usually the overthrow of an established government or way of life and its replacement by a new order along different lines.

Guerrilla activity is almost certain to arise as a result of some form of latent grievance or discontent against an established order. Racial and ethnic divides are always prime sources of discontent in any society, and industrial unrest is another rich vein of potential trouble. Guerrillas will channel that discontent to attract new recruits, gradually broadcasting the message that something is going to be done to change things. If there is no reason why the general population should feel any particular sense of grievance, the guerrillas may try to create a grievance. This may be done by issuing demands that cannot readily be met, insisting that changes are made here, there and everywhere, and openly establishing a general feeling of discontent and latent unrest. In almost every case the established authorities will either ignore such demands or go out of their way to deny them. The scene is then set for the next stage.

The second stage usually starts quietly and ends violently. In urban areas it commences with rallies, often fronted by legitimate or innocent notables, which then proceed to marches and finally end with riots. In the country, much the same path is followed, but definite acts of violence such as attacks on symbols of authority (local government officials, police stations, post offices, etc.) are carried out on a small scale quite early on. Headline-grabbing stunts such as airliner hijackings can provide publicity and help to broadcast the guerrillas' 'message'.

In most cases the response is some form of repressive security clamp-down. All too many governments find it necessary to use force in varying forms at an early stage in attempting to prevent unrest spreading further. That is precisely what the guerrilla leader usually wants, for the result will almost inevitably be a rising tide of resentment from those having to suffer the effects of the security measures involved. Human nature being what it is, the resentment is likely to be directed against the authorities rather than the guerrillas. More and more hitherto passive individuals will then find reason to join or support the guerrillas.

Once with the guerrillas, the recruits will be armed, trained and set loose, under the close control of the leader or his staff, to carry out the next stage of guerrilla activity, normally a gradual escalation of attacks of all kinds, ranging from the ambushing of individuals to large-scale raids on banks (to obtain funds) and military posts and installations (to obtain weapons and supplies). Further fund-raising efforts may include drug-trafficking, the running of illegal drinking or gambling dens, 'protection money' demands, and other lucrative criminal activities.

Seemingly random bombings are another standard part of any guerrilla activity. Any authoritarian attempts to repress the 'movement' are likely to result in yet more recruits or converts to the 'cause'. Any guerrilla or innocent casualties of government action will become 'martyrs', causing yet more resentment and unrest, while funerals of the 'martyrs' can be converted into political demonstrations. The scale gradually escalates to the point of open violence and insurrection and the overthrow of the government. The guerrillas then take over the role of government and the objective is achieved.

Of course, it is not always like that. The above simplistic scenario mentions only the overthrow of a government. Many guerrilla movements have been devoted to throwing out an invader, such as the overthrow of the German occupation forces in Yugoslavia by the partisan movement, or the attempts of the Polisario to throw out the Moroccans from the Western Sahara. Other scenarios exist, perhaps none more odd than the continuing internecine guerrilla warfare normally carried out among the population of Afghanistan. If they were not busy using guerrilla tactics in attempts to speed the occupying Soviet armed forces out of their country, they would be busy carrying out all manner of guerrilla activities amongst and against each other. To Afghan males, such activities are no more than the usual order of things.

So far, no mention has made of any time-scale. Some guerrilla movements have taken years to organize, and the first stage is often difficult to transform into the second. Such difficulties can give rise to the most unwelcome aspect of guerrilla tactics, namely the adoption of terror methods. These usually take the form of random bombing of civilian targets, the taking of hostages and the seemingly random murder of selected public figures. Any police or security force finds it extremely difficult to counter what often seem to be aimless terror activities, and it is all too easy to use the terms 'criminal' or 'terrorist' to mask the truth of what is really happening, which is usually a desperate attempt to create the disorder and social uproar in which guerrillas can thrive. Many highly-motivated guerrilla movements overdo the use of terror to such an extent that their lethal activities become counter-productive, and reach the point where their objectives are rejected by the vast mass of the local population. The guerrillas involved are soon either given away, or caught by the authorities. Many potential urban guerrillas have learned to their cost that their attempts to amplify high-flown political 'messages' by sheer terrorism have no chance of influencing anyone other than the mentally unbalanced or the hopelessly naïve.

In many countries the early stages of instigating the social unrest that the guerrilla requires are made only too easy by the nature of the government concerned or their policies. In many countries, basic human rights still count for little, while major social injustices, including the lack of any form of fair ownership of property (such as land), are openly flaunted. Such countries are ripe for the attentions of the guerrilla, and in such environments guerrillas are kept under a semblance of control only by the employment of overwhelming force in the form of police, paramilitary units (including locally-levied militias) and regular troops. Even the most highly-motivated and determined guerrilla cannot operate in the face of overwhelming odds. Thus, when confronted by superior counter-forces, guerrillas must go to ground, hiding or merging with the local population. Time spent in hiding can be devoted to recruitment, training, planning and preparation for the time when the pressure is relaxed, when guerrilla activities can start afresh. It should not be forgotten that in guerrilla warfare, the guerrilla nearly always holds the initiative. He chooses his time and place of operations, and he chooses to operate how and where he will gain maximum advantage with a minimum of effort.

Despite the success of numerous guerrilla movements over the years, many have been defeated. Many defeat themselves by setting hopelessly unrealistic objectives, such as attempting to establish Marxist regimes in countries where the greater part of the populace is comfortably well-off, well-fed and well-housed and where the government is established and relatively well supported. Every attempt to initiate guerrilla movements in such countries has come to naught, the only exception perhaps being Northern Ireland, which even the most involved observer will recognize as being a special case, and one where the guerrillas' stated objectives are as far away as ever.

Other guerrilla movements have been defeated only by prolonged and difficult campaigning by security forces. The best
counter to any guerrilla activity is intelligence, with both a small
and large 'i'. Knowledge of how, where and when guerrilla activities are going to take place is essential for counter-guerrilla
forces to operate successfully. Such information is only obtained
by long-term overt and covert observation, the gathering and
processing of all manner of information and the use of informers.
The guerrilla leader is only too well aware of the use of such
counter-ploys, and always attempts to operate accordingly, often
by using a 'closed cell' system. The importance of information
derived from informers is witnessed by the intense dread within
any guerrilla organization of 'traitors' and 'spies', and the dire
punishments dealt out to anyone suspected or proved to be passing information to the authorities. The use of the rubber tyre
and petrol 'necklace' in the South African townships, and of
electric drills for the IRA's kneecapping punishment, are grim examples of the type of punishment contemplated by guerrilla
organizations for use against those who are suspected of
treachery.

Perhaps the most obvious counter to any guerrilla movement
is the removal of the reasons that motivate and support guerrilla
activity. This is far easier said than done, for the determined
guerrilla will always attempt to create some form of discontent.
Yet in many countries, even a slight movement towards social or
land-owning equality may do much to remove the possibility of
guerrilla forces becoming firmly established.

Where organized guerrilla movements become established, the
simplest counter-ploy is to remove the environment in which the
guerrilla operates. This can vary from counter-productive ex-
tremes, such as the defoliation of large areas of South Vietnam
by the Americans, or the rounding up of Boer families into con-
centration camps by the British in the latter stages of the Second
Boer War. Far more effective was the long-term 'hearts and
minds' campaign carried out by the British in Malaya during the
early 1950s. That campaign effectively removed much of the support upon which the Communist-inspired Chinese guerrillas
relied in order to survive in a hostile landscape.

The above is a brief outline of the nature of the guerrilla and
his activities. In every instance, there are exceptions and

qualifications, but the basic outline is true for most cases. Whatever his motivation, though, the guerrilla must rely upon weapons to carry out his activities, either for self defence or to attack. It is time to study the weapons involved.

One important point has to be borne in mind when the contents of this book are read: almost throughout, the male term is used to describe the guerrilla. In nearly all guerrilla movements, however, both urban and rural, the female has an important role to play, to the point where women fight and operate alongside men on equal terms. Guerrilla warfare is one aspect of conflict where the female is every bit as deadly as the male. It should also be remembered that many guerrilla organizations actively encourage children of all ages to become involved in guerrilla activity, including the bearing of arms.

GENERAL NOTES ON GUERRILLA WEAPONS

Before delving into the details of guerrilla weapons, it would be as well to make a few general observations. One is that the guerrilla will use whatever weapons he can lay his hands on. This will vary from the use of simple kitchen knives to sophisticated guided missiles. The overall objective of the guerrilla, as in any form of warfare, is to destroy the enemy. Exactly how that is achieved is secondary to the means involved.

There are certain strictures, however, on the types of weapon guerrillas can employ. By their very nature, urban and rural guerrillas rely extensively upon mobility: any weapons therefore have to be portable, so ruled out right away are weapons such as coventional artillery. Hand-held weapons are the rule. The only large weapons involved have to be disguised in some form, e.g. car or suitcase bombs, or else have to be used in remote areas where scrutiny is unlikely, e.g. recoilless rifles and mortars in areas of Afghanistan or the jungles of Vietnam.

The second stricture is that weapons have to be concealed. Only in the latter stages of a guerrilla movement, or in areas far from the influence of authority, can weapons be carried or displayed openly. By their very nature, effective hand-held weapons are large. The only relatively small hand-held weapons are very close range weapons, such as pistols and sub-machine guns, that are virtually useless at other than point blank distances from a target.

Any weapon is designed to be just that – a weapon. It is very difficult to disguise an assault rifle as anything other than an assault rifle. Despite the use of folding butts, and the ability to be stripped down into small component parts, nearly all guerrilla weapons are difficult to conceal, and the very sight of something resembling a weapon is sufficient to give away a guerrilla to security forces. This is, of course, nothing new. Even knives, the oldest of guerrilla weapons, are difficult to hide about the person, and the most superficial body search will soon reveal the presence of a hidden blade. The mere fact that it is hidden is enough to give rise to suspicion, and the discovery or sight of a pistol or any other firearm will give rise to much more than just suspicion.

The only recourse open to the guerrilla is not to carry any weapon until it is required: thus the importance of the arms dump and the weapons courier to guerrilla operations. Many security forces rely heavily on searches for weapons caches, and any loss of weapons is usually a blow to guerrilla operations. The fact is that in any normal society, weapons of any kind are very difficult to obtain. These days there are few law-abiding societies that allow weapons to be purchased and carried openly, and even fewer that condone their indiscriminate use, even for hunting or other sporting purposes. Even simple restrictions, such as the use of firearms licences or permits, can hinder those requiring weapons for criminal or guerrilla purposes, although many successful guerrilla movements have nevertheless relied heavily on the use of sporting weapons and shotguns during the early stages of their operations.

Guerrillas must resort to one of several options to obtain weapons to arm themselves. One is the purchase of weapons from the criminal fraternity. In any society, criminals somehow manage to find someone who will supply them with guns with which to carry out their activities, and the guerrilla usually has recourse to similar outlets. The main problem is that such supply methods are very expensive, and unless a guerrilla movement has a good supply of money, the guerrillas themselves have to use criminal methods to obtain funds. Bank raids, kidnapping, the drug trade, and sheer banditry are among the more common guerrilla fund-raising methods. Raising money by appeals to sympathetic groups or populations rarely produces enough funds to finance anything but the most low-key of guerrilla activity.

A second supply method is the theft of weapons from local security forces, relying on the old guerrilla adage, 'if you have a knife, you can obtain a sword. If you have a sword you can obtain a rifle...' and so on. What the adage does not specify is how the obtaining is done. In practice, it involves the ambushing of individual soldiers or policemen and removal of their weapons by force. It sounds easy, but is far from being so. Security forces rarely lay themselves open to such forms of attack. Nor do they lay themselves open to that other guerrilla weapons supply method, namely the attack on installations where weapons are stored. Only carefully planned and executed raids on weapons stores can succeed, even when such attacks are not anticipated by the authorities. Even the most lax quartermaster keeps weapons locked away under strict security conditions at all times. Breaking into any gunroom is no easy matter, and the same can usually be said of explosives stores.

Then there is the international arms market. Throughout the world, there is a seemingly never-ending trade in arms that is quite separate from the well-publicized and open trade in new weapons. This is the realm of the second-hand dealers, who sell arms to all comers, but it should not be confused with the perfectly legitimate trade that is still a thriving part of the arms business. Many nations sell their old or obsolete weapons (or unwanted captured weapons stocks) to established dealers, who then openly and legally sell them to others. Their business is above-board, legal and open to any form of scrutiny. Most of the concerns involved are very careful about whom they sell to, and would be unwilling to sell weapons to any organizations that even smell of guerrilla activity.

Unfortunately, there are other arms dealers who are not so fussy: they will see to whoever will buy. Old or obsolete weapons are all that might be on offer, but such may be perfectly adequate for guerrilla use. As long as the money on the table is sufficient, guerrillas will always be able to obtain weapons from such merchants. Prices involved are high, delivery is often uncertain, and the goods are frequently of low quality, but if the guerrillas cannot obtain weapons from any other source, the shady side of the arms trade is always there to provide their requirements - at a price.

There are a few countries with nationally-owned and run arms production facilities which are happy to sell brand new weapons to whoever will buy, with no questions asked. It could be inviduous to name the nations involved, but even a perfunctory scrutiny of many of the weapons used by guerrilla organizations all around the world will soon reveal certain national indentities that are frequently repeated.

In the last resort, guerrillas can always attempt to produce their own weapons. Despite the considerable outlay of effort and expenditure involved, many guerrilla movements have had no alternative in the past, and have established what became large-scale production facilities based on the use of the back-street workshop and the jungle clearing assembly-line. Of course, not every guerrilla organization can aspire to such achievements. Many simply lack the opportunity, skills or facilities to undertake any scale of weapons production but most seem able to establish some form of production capability for explosives and explosive devices, along with the assembly of the timing systems involved. That, however, is the limit, for a good many guerrilla organizations. Only the largest and best established can produce weapons such as hand grenades and land mines, very few can attempt to produce items such as guns and ammunition: only the well-established workshops along the North-West Frontier between Pakistan and Afghanistan can achieve that, although the back-street armourers of Belfast have produced mortars and rudimentary sub-machine guns.

Even when guns and explosives are in the hands of the guerrilla, the supply problems do not cease. Any firearm is useless without ammunition, and any explosive is useless without some form of detonator or fuzing system to set it off. Dealing with firearms first, the supply of ammunition is usually far more difficult than the supply of firearms. Even in these days of ammunition standardization, there is still a wide array of ammunition types, to the point where even certain types of identical calibre ammunition will be unsuitable for some weapons. For instance, 7.62 mm NATO rounds cannot be fired from 7.62 mm AK-47 rifles. Bearing in mind the number of types of weapon any guerrilla movement might find itself having to use, supply problems can become major obstacles during operations.

Obtaining ammunition is often yet more difficult when the supply route is via criminal sources. The criminal usually requires only a few rounds to carry out his activities, but the guerrilla needs a large supply. Even the procurement by theft route is fraught with difficulty, for one of the basic security measures in any weapons store is that weapons and ammunition are stored separately, usually in different premises. Ammunition supply is thus a major problem for any guerrilla leader even when firearms are relatively plentiful.

The same goes for explosives. Guerrillas can rely upon several supply routes for explosives, ranging from surreptitious purchase or raiding quarries, to production in clandestine workshops. The main problem is detonating the explosive: that requires sophisticated and involved detonators of one form or another, and timing mechanisms are an extra complication. Guerrillas rarely use the old black powder and lit fuze type of bomb these days; plastic and commercial explosives are more favoured, as they produce much more chemical energy than the old types, are less bulky and are much more reliable in use. Their main drawback is their demand for detonators. Needless to say, most security-conscious authorities keep the supply and storage of such items under extremely strict controls.

Unfortunately for those who like a quiet life, there is a further and widely-used weapons supply route, and that is via friendly or like-minded states. Throughout the world there are a number of regimes which owe their establishment to revolutionary guerrilla activities, for whom the guerrilla is a method of spreading their particular political gospel or creed; several such nations come readily to mind. Those nations are apparently willing to extend aid of all kinds to other revolutionary guerrilla movements, and in the past several nations have openly provided 'approved' guerrilla organizations with weaponry of all kinds, frequently with no apparent strings attached. Some nations go so far as to offer training courses for selected personnel. Just as important are funds, which are sometimes provided open-handed by nations who do not wish to dirty their hands with weapons supply. With such benefactors around, it is not surprising that guerrilla movements have mushroomed over recent years.

Whatever the supply route, the division between urban and rural guerrilla factions gives rise to differing methods of using weapons. In guerrilla warfare there are no hard and fast rules, but generally speaking the urban guerrilla relies heavily on the use of bombs or grenades, explosive and/or incendiary, while his rural counterpart relies upon firearms and land mines.

The bomb or hand grenade can be a selective or random device. In either case the potential end result is the same; a considerable amount of destruction for only a limited outlay in effort, material and personal risk to the guerrilla. Timing and other devices make the bomb-type device safe to use by the guerrilla, and numerous methods can be employed to make the device as destructive and lethal as possible.

In terror situations, the use of firearms can be every bit as effective as a bomb. The mere sight of a determined guerrilla appearing armed in a crowded environment is enough to cause all manner of panic and dismay in any crowd. If the weapon involved is something as menacing in appearance as an assault rifle or sub-machine gun, the effect of its appearance alone can be every bit as extreme as the weapon firing; even the sight of a pistol can have a numbing effect on group behaviour. The outbreak of shooting from PLO guerrillas at Athens airport several years ago created mass panic that was every bit as welcome to the guerrillas who had planned and organized the attack as were the casualties produced by the shooting. That event created an air of apprehension and uncertainty among the travelling public, which extended far from Athens itself.

Shooting situations in rural areas are unlikely to have the same mass impact. Spaces are more open and ranges are likely to be greater. Rifles, and especially assault rifles, are more likely to be used than sub-machine guns. The assault rifle combines the combat range attributes of the conventional rifle with attributes of the automatic sub-machine gun.

Heavier weapons such as the machine gun, mortar and recoilless rifle are rarely encountered in urban guerrilla situations. The knowledge that a guerrilla organization has such weapons can be both unsettling to the security authorities, who might expect to be on the receiving end, and encouraging to the guerrillas involved, but all too often the ownership of heavy weapons by guerrillas can be counter-productive. If ever a heavy weapon is employed operationally by guerrillas, it becomes something that has to be protected. Obtaining such a weapon entails time, effort and money. Once shown in public, it possesses considerable propaganda clout, but that often means that guerrillas have to stand and fight in order to gain time for the precious machine gun (or whatever) to be spirited away every time it is used. Rapidly hiding something as large and conspicuous as a heavy machine gun is not easy. The result has often been fire-fights with security forces who are far better equipped and able to conduct such clashes than the guerrillas. Thus guerrillas can become casualties, often leading to the loss not only of the prestigious heavy weapon, with all its subsequent propaganda value to the security forces, but also to the loss of trained guerrilla personnel and their personal weapons.

In really remote areas such as Afghanistan, such drawbacks rarely apply. There the use of heavy machine guns, mortars and recoilless rifles by the Mujahadeen is commonplace. There is sufficient unpatrolled open country between the few roads for the

Mujahadeen to quite openly carry and use heavy weapons including, it should not be forgotten, portable ground-to-air
missiles such as Stinger and Blowpipe. Africa is another area
where similar weapons can be openly deployed by guerrilla
forces.

In more heavily-populated areas the use of heavy weapons
such as missiles is likely to be limited to one-off attacks involving
the firing of missiles against aircraft, followed by the immediate
going to ground of the guerrillas involved. In these conditions
mortars, including home-made mortars, become one-shot
weapons that are less effective than bombs, yet more demanding
in effort to produce and deploy.

The same cannot be said for the shoulder-launched anti-
armour rocket weapons now employed by many guerrilla forces,
however. Weapons such as the RPG-7 and M72 rocket launchers are relatively small, easy to use and are highly portable.
They are also dreadfully effective against armoured targets of all
kinds, from blockhouses to armoured vehicles. At the same time,
though, they are extremely noisy, have a very short range, kick
up clouds of revealing dust when fired, and sometimes require
the firer to expose himself to view at the moment of launch, so
they are far from being ideal guerrilla weapons.

The array of weapons now available to the guerrilla should not
obscure one important aspect of their use: any weapon is only as
good as the person who uses it. Mere ownership of a
sophisticated weapon does not automatically bestow the full
potential of that weapon on the user. Any complicated weapon
requires care in its handling, training to obtain its full potential,
and maintenance to keep it serviceable. In guerrilla organizations, all three of these requirements are likely to be missing,
with training the most important missing item. Very often it
would appear that weapons are simply handed out to whoever is
available, so even the potential of a comparatively simple
weapon such as an assault rifle is lost through lack of any training. Rudimentary skills such as aiming are often neglected to the
point where recruits have to learn by directly copying others
who have been around longer, and if the recruit notices that the
more experienced user closes his eyes as the trigger is pulled, the
recruit may feel constrained to do likewise. The result is the type
of ammunition-wasting blasting off into the blue that is apparent
on newsreels from the Lebanon and Southern Africa. When

such wastage is combined with a lack of proper maintenance, the result is often an unserviceable weapon. One wonders how some of the more primitive guerrilla groups manage to look after weapons such as Stinger or SA-7 air defence missiles.

Of course, not all guerrillas are ignorant of the basics of weapon usage and care: many are as accomplished with the weapons at their disposal as any of the security operatives arrayed against them - more so, in some situations. Once they have been given a course of training and have gained some experience, determined guerrillas are a menace to any society. They are determined and motivated to achieve an objective, often an intangible idea or concept. History has shown many times that the power of an idea can be far greater than any of the physical forces and weapons disposed against it. One of the major mistakes that security forces commonly make when dealing with guerrilla forces is to underestimate their ability and will to fight. History is littered with those who have made that mistake and paid for it dearly.

EXPLOSIVE DEVICES

Among the most versatile and effective weapons used by guerrillas are those which are explosive in some form or another. They vary from the simple blast weapons, formed by setting off blocks of explosive, to sophisticated devices such as limpet and anti-tank mines. Closely allied are the incendiaries, that rely upon inflammability for their destructive effect, and they will be considered in this section, along with booby traps.

Explosives

Explosives come in many forms. They vary mainly in their chemical composition and the energy levels produced when they are detonated. The energy produced by an explosive is derived from the rapid release of chemical energy at the instant of detonation, mainly in the form of heat. The heat produced causes the atmosphere surrounding the explosion to expand at such a rate that blast pressure waves are produced, with

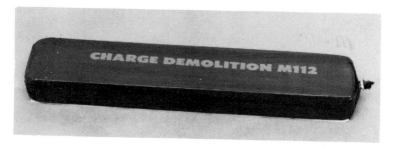

Above *A typical military demolition charge, the American Charge Demolition M112 which weighs 0.567 kg. Many producers outside the United States simply copy American specifications for their own demolition products.*

Right *A selection of demolition charges produced by Cardoen of Chile.*

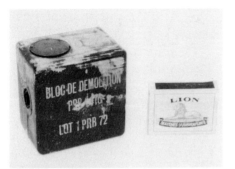

Left *A 400 gram block of Trialene, produced by PRB of Belgium as their NR 416 demolition charge, that showhow turned up in Angola (D. Radmore).*

Left *The Soviet SZ-3 demolition charge is contained in a light metal container (D. Radmore).*

Below *A Soviet SZ-6 demolition charge (D. Radmore).*

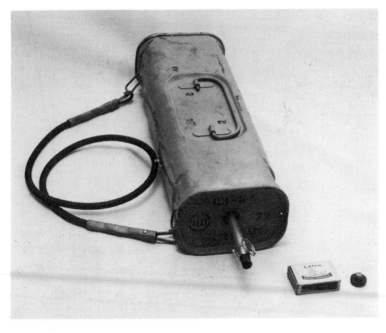

attendant damage-producing effects. Secondary effects are flash, noise, and, in many cases, the heat itself, which can cause extra incendiary damage.

Guerrillas tend to use whatever explosives they can lay their hands on. If they can get them, military explosives, specially produced for destructive or demolition purposes, are preferable. If they cannot obtain such specialized explosives, then the forms of explosive used for quarrying or similar civilian construction projects are almost as effective as their military counterparts. If none of those are available, then recourse has to be made to producing explosives in back-yard workshops.

Specialized military explosives come in many forms. Most are used for demolishing structures such as bridges, or for producing obstacles to movement, such as craters. Others are used as cutting charges to cut through metal or concrete structures. Most military explosives produce large amounts of chemical energy for the relatively small volumes involved. TNT (trinitrotoluene) is a typical military explosive although there are many others. For demolition purposes, TNT is issued in prepared blocks or cylinders that vary in weight from 250 grammes up to monster quantities weighing 50kg or more. The TNT is usually covered by a protective medium such as metal foil, plastic, or thin metal, to prevent moisture damage, but every form of container has provision for inserting a detonator. Some blocks also have an integral booster to assist detonation.

For straightforward blast production, explosive blocks are simply placed in position and a detonator is inserted. The detonator can then be initiated by a small electrical current, by chemical means or some other method. The chemical method could involve a delay device known as a time pencil, in which acid eats its way through a soft metal spring or strip. When the metal has dissolved the explosive is set off either by further chemical action, or via a form of percussion device known as a blasting cap. If required, the explosive can be detonated directly by percussion means, using a special form of detonator. In the absence of anything else, recourse could be made to a slow-burning fuze known as detonating cord, connected to a special detonator.

Whatever method is used, the result is an explosion that destroys structures or materials, and the resultant blast wave produces more potentially casualty-producing effects by blasting

Above *The Charge Linear Cutting is produced by Royal Ordance in the United Kingdom and is typical of many similar specialist shaped charges used to cut through steel and other materials; the charge can be cut and shaped to suit the user.*

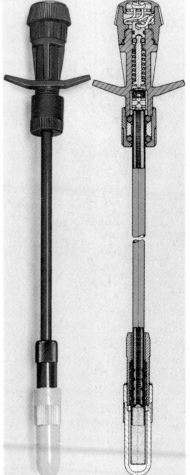

Right *West German firing devices used to detonate explosive charges after a time delay; on the left is the DM 121, which has a 15 second delay, while the DM111 (right) has a 60-second delay.*

debris about. Some guerrillas enhance these blast and debris effects by the deliberate packing of metal or other small projectiles around the explosive block. The infamous nail bomb is simply an explosive block surrounded by clusters of ordinary steel nails held in position by adhesive tape; the anti-personnel effects can be dreadful.

Less frequently used by guerrillas are cutting charges. These are specialized charges that embody the hollow charge principle, in which a block of explosive has a concave conical depression set into one side or end. As the charge is detonated the energy produced tends to concentrate in the concave depression and is directed away from the depression in a very hot, thin jet of heat or flame. This jet can literally burn its way through metal or concrete to considerable depths, depending on the type and initial weight of explosive involved, the shape and size of the cone, and so on. The hollow charge principle is also used for some commercial construction purposes.

Less used for commercial purposes are plastic explosives, or PX. These are much favoured by many guerrilla movements, for many reasons. Most plastic explosives have the appearance and handling properties of plasticine, and are just as safe to handle as that innocuous substance, until a detonator is introduced to the plastic explosive and initiated. It then explodes, producing high energy levels. In its normal state plastic explosive is very stable and can be moulded or cut to shape, sawn, thrown about and generally treated completely unlike any other form of explosive. It can be produced in sheet, strip, cylinder or block form, and is usually odourless and non-toxic.

As with other types of explosive, there are many forms of plastic explosive. Many involve the use of a conventional explosive known as RDX, combined with a plastic polymer.

Commercial explosives are widely used in activities such as quarrying and during large-scale construction projects. The classic explosive used is dynamite, based originally on the use of nitro-glycerine, a substance once well respected for its instability and for its tendency to detonate when jarred. Modern dynamites are now very stable and some make no use of nitro-glycerine at all. They generally tend to be relatively slow-burning explosives, and have a correspondingly lower chemical energy output. They are much used to produce craters and to blast through large quantities of earth, so are sometimes known as 'heaving' explosives. Dynamite, if detonated in the right place and at the right time, can be every bit as destructive as the more powerful military explosives, so to the guerrilla, dynamite is invaluable. It is also relatively easy to obtain or steal from commercial explosive stores. Consequently much use is made of commercial explosives in the construction of culvert mines and in the general mining of roads and tracks for ambushes.

As has already been mentioned, where no other form of explosive is available, explosives can be produced by guerrillas themselves. The production and handling of any explosive is no easy matter, and can be extremely dangerous. There is also the problem that many home-made explosives are prone to chemical and physical instability, and can be just as dangerous to the user as to the target. The main problem for security forces attempting to deal with home-made explosives is that the basic ingredients of many home-produced explosive substances are commonplace and can be found in many households or communities without difficulty and without having to obtain restricted materials (other than the detonators). This book is not going to outline what those ingredients are.

Home-produced explosives are of relatively low energy and have to be used in large amounts to produce worthwhile destructive explosions: hence the multi-hundred kilogram bombs discovered or used in culvert mines in Northern Ireland and elsewhere. The explosive is usually packed into containers such as beer kegs, milk churns or vehicles.

The car bomb is nothing new, being little else than a method of delivering large amounts of explosive to a target area in a mobile disguise. Once in position, a timing device or some other means of detonation is initiated and the driver leaves the area. In extreme cases, such as during the recent disturbances in Lebanon, the car bomb driver has seemingly been pleased to set the device off suicidally by his own direct and fleeting initiation of the detonation process.

Most car bomb detonations are aimed at material damage, since security forces are usually on the look-out for such devices and areas can be rapidly cleared if one is spotted or suspected, but occasionally they are deliberately used to inflict casualties (again, the Lebanon provides many examples), more usually in locations where car bombs are novel or unexpected devices. The car bomb is really a terrorist device that is meant to cause uncertainty and disruption on a large scale.

Grenades

In some guerrilla organizations, the hand grenade is virtually a symbol of guerrilla activity. Many revolutionary movements produce posters or literature in which a hand holding aloft a hand grenade is a standard illustration of determination and commitment, which is not really surprising, for in many ways the hand grenade is an ideal guerrilla weapon.

The grenade is an ancient military weapon that has enjoyed a resurgence of use during the last century. It exists today in two main forms, offensive and defensive, but both are offensive in their employment, if not in nature. In its offensive form the grenade is used as an attacking weapon to produce fragments and blast. In its defensive form the grenade produces only flash, noise, and a minimum of dangerous fragments.

The latter is meant to stun, blind and generally bewilder

Below *The venerable No 36M 'Mills Bomb', a grenade typical of the old type, with an externally-serrated cast steel or iron body that did nothing to improve fragmentation.*

Below Right *Typical of the more modern type of hand grenade is the Chilean FAMAE GM 78-F7. This plastic-bodied grenade can be fitted with a coil of notched steel wire to produce fragments and may also be fitted with a pressure plate to form a small anti-personnel mine (T. Gander).*

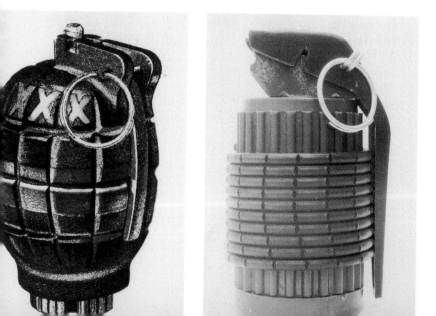

(hence the term 'stun grenade') and is largely used by counter-guerrilla forces in situations where the taking of prisoners is an objective, or in situations where hostages are involved. Such grenades are rarely used by guerrillas, other than in situations where they wish to spread confusion or sheer terror.

The classic form of offensive hand grenade is the 'pineapple' grenade on which the metal body (usually cast steel or iron) is serrated on its outer surface to produce fragments when detonated, or such was the theory. Examples of these are the Soviet Model F1, the American Mk 2A1 and the British No.36M 'Mills Bomb'. Despite their obsolescence, all three of these grenades are still widely favoured by many guerrilla organizations, and where original examples cannot be procured, they are copied and produced in back-street workshops and foundries.

The factor of obsolescence has been brought about by the discovery that serrating the outside of the grenade body makes no difference to fragment production. To produce fragments of controlled size, the serrations have to be machined or cast inside the body, which makes them difficult to produce. It is far easier to pack the grenade bodies with coils or strips of pre-notched wire next to the main explosive charge. The result is a large number of lethal fragments which can remain dangerous out to a range of 25 metres or more from the point of explosion, far more than the 10 metres or so of the older designs.

Guerrillas find it more difficult to manufacture these more modern pre-notched or pre-serrated grenades. Many resort to producing nothing more complex than a block of explosive surrounded by nails or metal scrap, usually in a tin or simply taped to the explosive block. Other widely-favoured home-made grenades use sections of closed pipe packed with explosive and fitted with rudimentary firing devices.

When guerrillas do have access to the more modern grenades, they may end up with some very lethal devices. Many modern grenades do not have metal bodies, but are plastic-bodied defensive grenades. By fitting a coil of pre-notched steel wire around the body, however, an offensive grenade is produced. This simple approach has many attractions to guerrillas, for it requires very little imagination to see that there are several variations on this theme. By replacing the usual lever and delay fusing system with a pull or pressure igniter, the same grenade can be converted into the basis of a booby trap, and fitting a pressure sensor will produce a small land mine.

In production terms, hand grenades are relatively simple to manufacture by methods available to many guerrilla organizations. They are small, easy to conceal, easy to use, and are lethal to an extreme. They can also be produced to meet particular local requirements.

One example of the latter can be seen in Northern Ireland, where the security forces make considerable use of lightly-armoured vehicles for their own protection when travelling through certain areas of the Province, and the IRA has produced a special armour-penetrating grenade to attack such vehicles. Their grenade is a rough copy of the Soviet RPG-43, which was first produced during the Second World War. In military terms the RPG-43 is obsolete, but is still more than capable of penetrating the protection of the armoured Land Rovers and other vehicles used by the Northern Ireland security forces. The IRA might have had a few RPG-43s at one time, but when they were gone they decided to produce their own version, using tin cans for the body and plastic explosive with an indentation to produce a hollow charge effect on the open end. To ensure that the hollow charge would impinge upon the target armour correctly the rudimentary throwing handle had a number of strips of cloth attached to stream out to the rear when thrown, to keep the grenade body facing the target.

Another Soviet grenade that is very similar to the RPG-43 is the RPG-6, which is still widely encountered in guerrilla hands. To continue such a litany of possible hand grenade types is not possible in a book of this size: the list would simply be too long. Suffice to say that anything from Second World War stick grenades to the most modern miniature plastic-bodied grenades might be found in use. However, there are two further types of grenade to consider. One of these is the rifle grenade, a weapon still widely used by the armed forces of many nations. The main attraction of the rifle grenade is that it has a combat range much greater than the hand-delivered grenade. The drawback is that it usually requires special ammunition to be fired from a launcher located on the muzzle of a standard service rifle. For some guerrilla groups the provision of another form of special ammunition, and perhaps a detachable launcher as well, is yet another logistical difficulty. The rifle grenade also takes skill and training to use accurately, while the manufacture of such weapons is usually beyond the scope of most guerrillas' back-street workshops. Consequently, the rifle grenade is nowhere near as popular as the hand grenade, with many guerrilla organizations.

One grenade weapon that would be more widely employed by many guerrillas, if they had the chance, is the grenade cartridge, an American innovation first used in quantity during the Vietnam campaigns. This type of grenade is fired from a special launcher, in much the same way as an orthodox cartridge is used in a rifle or shotgun. A small propelling charge projects a small grenade to ranges of up to 400 metres or so, although combat ranges are much lower (about 150 metres is the usual with launchers such as the American M203, mentioned later in this section). American grenades in this class have a calibre of 40 mm; their Soviet equivalents have a calibre of 30 mm. On target, these small grenades have a lethal radius of only five metres or so, due mainly to their small size, but they can be accurately delivered, and fully-automatic projectors such as the Soviet AGS-17 have been devised to make their impact even more effective. Various forms of grenade are produced for both 30 and 40 mm calibre. Most use simple high-explosive payloads, but others have high explosive fragmentation fillings, and attempts have been made to produce armour-piercing versions. Other payloads include CS riot control gas, flares, and various forms and colours of smoke.

The first launchers for these small grenades resembled oversize shotguns. Typical was the single-shot M79, an American

Early model of a 40 mm M79 grenade launcher (US Army).

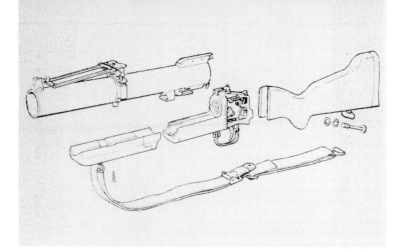

weapon. This had the disadvantage that it was a dedicated weapon, to the extent that when carrying it a soldier could not easily carry any other weapon. While this might not worry the average guerrilla unduly, it did worry many conventional soldiers. The result was the single-shot launcher, such as the American M203, that fits under the barrel of a standard assault rifle.

The combination of a rifle and a grenade launcher would seem to form an ideal weapon for the guerrilla, combining as it does the capability of a direct fire aimed weapon and an area fire support weapon. When the Americans left Vietnam, they left behind large stocks of 40 mm grenades and their launchers, so their use is now fairly widespread by regular and irregular forces throughout South-East Asia.

Similar weapons to the American 40 mm grenades have turned up in Afghanistan, but they are ex-Soviet 30 mm grenades and their launchers. Most of them have been captured from the occupying Soviet forces, including both the belt-fed automatic APG-17 *Plamya* (Flame) launchers, and a single-shot launcher that is very similar to the American M203 and fits under the barrel of the AK-74 assault rifle. Similar weapons have also turned up in parts of Southern Africa. As yet, the use of these grenades and their launchers has not been widespread elsewhere but, as they appear to be ideal guerrilla weapons for many applications, their future adoption by many guerrilla organizations seems certain, once they can get their hands on them.

Land mines

The land mine is a weapon that first came to prominence at the

Above Left *Cut-away of a 40 mm M79 grenade launcher.*

Above *Despite its age, the Soviet TM-38 anti-tank mine is still in use and has been encountered in Southern Africa. It was first produced in 1938 and has a main charge weighing 3.6 kg (T. Gander).*

Below *The TMA-2 anti-tank mine is produced in Yugoslavia and has a plastic body. The two fuzes are under the two circular covers (D. Radmore).*

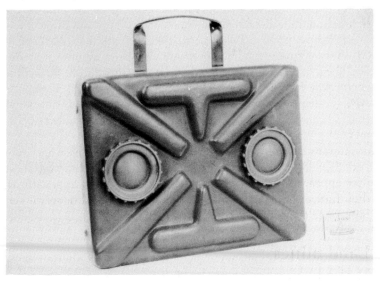

end of the First World War, and which saw large-scale use during the Second World War. It is now regarded as one of the few weapons that, when used correctly in large numbers, can slow down or stop the advance of large armoured forces, but it is equally effective in small numbers when used by guerrillas.

There are two main types of land mine, anti-tank and anti-personnel. A few other types exist, such as off-route mines and alarm mines, but they are special application weapons.

Anti-tank and anti-personnel mines are meant to be used in large numbers. Laid in large minefields, both types of mine are intended to slow down or prevent the large-scale movement of enemy forces, or else to channel those forces towards areas of the defenders' choosing. Used individually and thoughtfully, land mines become potent weapons for the guerrilla, as well.

The basic anti-tank mine is a simple device, being a block of explosive held in a container and detonated by a pressure fuze. The container can be metal, some form of plastic-based material, or wood. Some mines have glass containers. The metal-based mines are more easily detected by magnetic sensors such as mine detectors, but nearly all mines, both anti-personnel and anti-tank, contain at least a small amount of metal in the pressure fuze. The pressure fuze of an anti-tank mine is meant to be set off only by the weight of a vehicle, and will therefore not normally be set off by the weight of a man (although walking across anti-tank minefields is not a recommended practice). Most anti-tank mine fuzes are initiated by a weight of 175 kg or upwards, which means that they can only be detonated by trucks or similar vehicles, as well as tanks. Trucks and buses are far more likely to be targets for the guerrilla than tanks.

When detonated, most anti-tank mines rely upon sheer blast to produce damage. The usual explosive payload for most anti-tank mines is at least 7 kg, with TNT being a favoured filling. Setting off such a charge will be enough to blow off tank tracks and perhaps penetrate, or at least damage, belly armour. The effect on an unarmoured vehicle such as a truck or bus can be imagined.

To enhance their anti-armour effect, some anti-tank mines have upward-facing hollow charge warheads, while others use an effect known as the self-forming fragment. This employs a process whereby the explosive charge acts upon a specially-shaped sheet of metal (usually copper). As the explosive detonates, the resultant pressure waves form the metal sheet into a small, bullet-shaped fragment which is propelled upwards at extremely high velocity to punch its way through the target tank's belly armour.

The guerrilla can use anti-tank mines to great effect. They can be used to destroy vehicles in remote areas, so that the security forces involved will have to patrol or at least search the area concerned for more mines. Intermittent laying of mines along roads or tracks could involve security forces in prolonged, potentially dangerous and time-consuming detection and clearance operations, involving a great deal of manpower in the process, and possibly enabling the guerrillas to operate more freely elsewhere. Careful laying of anti-tank mines could lead to deliberate operations against selected security forces or other vehicles, and they could certainly be employed to considerable effect in ambush situations. The use of the anti-tank mine by guerrillas is seemingly limited only by the guerrillas' ingenuity and can only be countered by considerable investment in time, material and manpower resources by the security forces concerned. In Southern Africa the guerrilla anti-tank mine has been effectively countered only by the widespread adoption of mine-proof vehicles, and at considerable cost.

One of the most widely-adopted guerrilla anti-tank mines is the Soviet TM-46, along with the generally similar TMN-46, TM-57 and TM-62. All these metal-bodied circular mines have

The Soviet TMN-46 metal-cased anti-tank mine is used widely and can be fitted with an anti-lift device in the base; it contains 5.95 kg of explosive (D. Radmore).

The Soviet TM-46 metal-cased anti-tank mine is perhaps the most widely-encountered of all anti-tank mines in guerrilla use. It has been copied and manufactured by nations such as Bulgaria, China, Egypt and Israel. The main charge weighs 5.3 kg.

turned up in nearly every area of guerrilla activity, but not all the mines involved are of Soviet manufacture. All the mines mentioned above have been produced in nations such as Egypt, Israel, Bulgaria and China. Other nations producing anti-tank mines that are frequently encountered in guerrilla hands include Yugoslavia, Czechoslovakia and the United Kingdom. Most of the UK mines are old Mark 5 and Mark 7 models; both were extensively stockpiled at many old British Army bases in the past. They were also produced in many of the old Commonwealth countries, such as India. As Mark 5 and Mark 7 mines are now regarded as obsolete, many have been sold off on the open market, but have ended up in guerrilla armouries.

The land mine perhaps most suited to guerrilla operations is the wooden mine, epitomized by the Soviet TMB-D. This mine uses a simple wooden case that can be easily produced by guerrillas themselves using local materials. All they have to procure is the explosive filling. The TMD-B uses a standard detonator and igniter, while the pressure plate relies upon a wooden plank breaking under strain. It is simple, very effective and very difficult to detect by standard methods. The Soviet TMD-44 anti-tank mine also uses wood for its basic construction.

The anti-personnel mine is not usually laid in such large numbers as the anti-tank mine, and is often employed in ones and twos, mainly to delay and harass. Generally speaking, the

TMD-B anti-tank wooden mine

Above *Drawing of a typical TMD-B wooden-bodied anti-tank mine. These Soviet mines can be produced using local resources, so many variations abound. A typical charge could weigh up to 6.8 kg.*

Below *How the pressure device operates on a TMD-B wooden anti-tank mine. Pressure has to be maintained on the top surface to ensure that the wooden slat under the centre board breaks, the centre board then operates the fuze (D. Radmore).*

array of anti-personnel mine type is wider than that of anti-tank mines, and the number of operating principles involved is larger. They range from small and simple pressure-activated devices containing a small explosive charge, to trip-wire activated devices that propel a small projectile into the air to detonate at about mid-body height and spread a lethal circle of fragments. Then there are the claymore mines, which are little other than static shotguns, that fire their payload of metal balls set into an explosive matrix, over a defined arc, and the stake mines that are similar but spread their fragments over a full 360-degree arc.

Anti-personnel mines, whatever their activating sensor might be (pressure or trip-wire), can be detonated by very light pressures, often nothing more than a touch. They are very nasty devices. The explosive payloads in the pressure-activated versions are measured only in grams: such small charges can rarely kill, but can maim by blowing off feet or fingers. The fragment-producing anti-personnel mines are generally more lethal, especially the claymore mines, which can be dangerous out to ranges of 50 metres or so. Bounding mines use a pressure fuze or a trip-wire to set off a small charge inside the mine body, which is usually buried underground. The charge propels a small projectile (sometimes a modified hand grenade) vertically upwards, until a wire secured to the mine body is drawn taut to initiate the

Above Left *A Soviet TMD-44 anti-tank mine, another Soviet wooden-bodied mine* (D. Radmore).

Above *Another wooden-bodied mine, this time the Soviet PMD-57 anti-personnel mine* (D. Radmore).

Below *The business face of the American M18 claymore mine, seen here with its support legs folded.*

projectile fuze. The lethal radius of such mines can be of the order of 25 metres or more.

The number of models of all these mines is legion. Typical of the pressure-activated anti-personnel mines are the Soviet PMD-6 and PMD-7 mines. These use wooden boxes in which the 'lid' acts as the pressure plate. Treading on the lid will force it down, to operate a striker; the striker will then detonate the mine. Some designs are more sophisticated. The East German PPM-2 has a much more complex operating system. It has a flexible domed upper surface, and if this is depressed by pressure, an internal mechanism produces an electrical current to detonate the small explosive charge. The little American plastic-bodied M14 anti-personnel mine relies upon pressure only, and is widely used.

The best example of the claymore mine is the American M18. This is widely produced under licence (in Chile and South Korea for example – it is copied direct by South Africa) and often ends up in guerrilla hands. It can be fired by trip-wire or by remote control, and spreads 700 steel balls over an arc 60 degrees wide and up to 2 metres high.

One of the most widely-used of all the bounding mines is the Soviet OZM-3, along with its more modern version, the OZM -4. Their American equivalent is the M16 series of generally-similar bounding mines. Another type of anti-personnel mine is the stake mine, which consists of an explosive charge set inside a fragmentation sleeve and secured to a stake driven into the ground, usually just above ground surface. A typical example is the Soviet POZM-2 and its derivatives. Again, although these latter mines were originally of Soviet design, they are now produced widely by nations such as China, Yugoslavia and North Korea. Many other nations make similar mines, and the stake mine is simple enough to be produced in back-street workshops. The stake involved is often cut from a nearby tree just before the mine is emplaced.

The off-route mine was originally designed for use in ambushes or in built-up areas. It consists of a trip-wire or some form of pressure sensor device strung across or buried under a route, to fire some form of rocket or other projectile into the side of a passing vehicle. Similar devices can be produced by connecting standard shoulder-launched rocket launchers to some form of remote control or pressure device and can be invaluable in built-

The component parts of the Soviet POMZ-2 anti-personnel stake mine, usually detonated by trip wire (D. Radmore).

up areas, both as ambush and nuisance weapons.

Alarm mines are rarely used by guerrillas, since they are used to set off thunderflashes, flares or smoke pots when activated. As their designation implies, they are meant to produce alarms to warn of the approach of others – most guerrillas would rather use more lethal methods to warn of the approach of an enemy. If some form of sentinel alarm is required, the old and economical expedient of attaching tin cans to a wire is usually all that is necessary.

Limpet mines

The limpet mine is primarily an underwater weapon used by special forces personnel such as frogmen to attach explosive charges to the hulls of ships. Guerrillas have also found them very useful, however, for they usually have very high energy explosive charges. A relatively small limpet mine can produce a large explosion for its size.

Limpet mines use magnets for attachment to the hulls of ships, and the same magnets can clamp the mines just as securely to the sides of vehicles. As their use in South Africa has shown, the magnets can also be used to secure limpet mines to the interior or underside of litter bins or similar objects in public places or buildings. The resultant blasts have produced considerable

A Soviet SPM limpet mine (D. Radmore).

numbers of casualties. Limpet mines were used by the Vietcong, and they have also been employed in Central Asia.

The limpet mine is a relatively small device. A typical example is the Soviet SPM, a semi-cylindrical mine with a plastic body. The mine is held in position against its target by two horseshoe magnets so that the main charge (0.95 kg of an explosive known as Tritanol) is held in direct contact with the target. The fuze employed has a mechanical time delay, and can be set for any delay time from five minutes to 800 hours. One small point to indicate how efficient some guerrillas have become when using such mines is the cutting off of the mine's canvas carrying handle just before the mine is emplaced. Removing the handle makes the mine that much more difficult to remove if discovered.

The SPM is only one type of limpet mine in use by guerrillas. Another similar limpet mine that is frequently encountered in guerrilla hands is the British Clam Mark 111. Exactly where these surfaced from is unclear, but they have been used widely by guerrilla groups in Africa. Another Soviet limpet mine is the Type 158, which seems to be an exact copy of the British Clam mine.

Incendiary devices

Fire has always been a weapon of war, employed for everything from ending an enemy's life to destroying property, crops and material. Needless to say, it is one of the methods used by guerrillas to wage their particular kind of warfare, but quite apart from the expedient of simply setting fire to something, the guerrilla does employ some specialized incendiary weapons.

One of the most widely used of all guerrilla weapons is the device popularly known as the 'Molotov Cocktail'. This weapon was given its name during the Spanish Civil War (1936~39) when it was employed against Nationalist tanks by Republican combatants. In its simplest form the Molotov Cocktail is an ordinary glass bottle filled with petrol, with a petrol-soaked rag tied around the neck of the bottle. Just before use the rag is ignited and the bottle is then thrown at the target. On impact the bottle breaks and the rag sets light to the bottle's contents. The results are often spectacular, but relatively harmless, since petrol burns rapidly and little harm is likely to be done to the target, unless of course it happens to be of an inflammable nature.

During the Second World War the basic Molotov Cocktail design became more sophisticated. The burning rag fuze was done away with, and instead the petrol contained a suspension of white phosphorus or something similar to act as an igniter. Some practitioners also took to converting the basic petrol content into a thicker, more viscous fluid by adding substances such as thin latex and some form of soap. The resultant mixture could then adhere to a target as it burned, to produce better incendiary effects.

In all its forms the Molotov Cocktail is still a universal guerrilla weapon. It is simple to make and easy to use. However, it is only effective on inflammable targets. To destroy uninflammable material, something producing very high temperatures is required. This is the realm of the thermal charge, which can produce intense heat. Some forms of thermal charge require no oxygen to make them burn ~ they can even burn under water.

The basic material used is generally known as thermite, a variable mixture of iron oxide and aluminium powder. Thermite requires a high temperature to get it to start burning, but this can be produced by special detonators. Once thermite is burning, it can be virtually impossible to extinguish.

Thermal charges can burn at temperatures of up to 2,400°C, which means they can be used to weld metals together, or even to burn through metal. A typical military sabotage application is to introduce a thermal charge to the chamber of an artillery piece. Once the breech block is closed, the thermal charge can burn and weld it shut permanently, which provides an indication of the ferocity of the heat involved.

Simple forms of thermal charge can be produced in guerrilla workshops, but the special detonators are not easy to manufacture or come by. Various forms of thermal charge are produced for commercial purposes, and some military forces use them for special demolitions, so it is possible for thermal charges to come into guerrilla hands, via the usual supply routes, to become terrible weapons.

Various other forms of incendiary weapon are used by guerrilla forces. Some are produced by combining various inflammable materials with conventional or home-made explosives, to add to a device's overall destructive effects, while others have integral timing devices to burn down buildings in the middle of the night, when a fire might be least expected or countered, to give one possible instance of use. Other incendiary weapons are nothing more than explosive devices attached to containers of petrol, or mixtures of petrol and diesel or other oils, to produce horrific flame weapons with dreadful anti-personnel effects. When explosives are used in conjunction with butane or similar substances, the effects can be equally terrible.

Booby traps

In guerrilla warfare, the array of devices that come under the general heading of booby traps is so wide that they are virtually impossible to cover in a book of this nature. They vary from the simple pit dug in a path and covered for the unwary to fall into, to the rigging of dead bodies with sensor devices that detonate explosives as the body is approached or moved. In between are microswitches that operate some form of lethal device as a door is opened or a foot is placed on a board, telephones that explode as the handset is lifted, and vehicles carrying explosives that detonate as they are driven away from a stationary position. The letter or parcel bomb must not be forgotten, either.

All military forces use a variety of detonators and firing devices that rely upon an alteration of pressure or some other form of movement to make then initiate a lethal device, usually an explosive charge, although any of the explosive and incendiary devices covered in this section could be involved. Where such devices are not readily available, they can be improvised using a seemingly endless number of simple devices such as clothes pegs, springs, elastic bands and torch batteries – the list is limited only by the operative's ingenuity and imagination. Using such simple materials the guerrilla can manufacture booby-trap devices for use in any number of applications.

Once manufactured, booby-trap devices can be employed for a wide range of purposes. Innocuous objects can be left around for an approaching enemy to pick up or disturb – anything from cans of beer to bicycles come into this category – or explosive devices can be set off by the unwary stepping on sensors or moving objects such as windows or doors. The object is to keep an enemy always on alert and uncertain of what they might next encounter. Used with skill, booby traps can make even the most highly-trained security forces jumpy and suspicious to the point where they over-react to any slight provocation. Booby traps also make them ultra-cautious and slow down their operations.

There is also the terror effect. Once guerrillas, urban or rural, start to use booby traps against the population at large, there are usually demands for the security forces to take some form of action to stop such activities. Unfortunately any action is difficult to take, other than the stepping up of patrols, the use of checkpoints and searches and the general disruption of everyday life. In some areas, even the most basic security activity is impossible, due to the size or the nature of the country involved. Either way, the security forces come under criticism. Increasingly, the general population will be prevented from undertaking simple routine activities such as shopping or travelling, without coming into possible contact with all manner of booby-trap devices.

It takes only one or two booby-trap devices to be operated to make any community wary and uncertain. Thus the use of a few terrorist-type booby traps can make the job of the guerrilla a relatively easy task. In such circumstances, established government and security forces can be made to look very foolish and ineffective at the cost of only a few grams of explosive and a few simple home-made devices.

RIFLES AND SHOTGUNS

The main weapon of any armed force that fights on foot is the service rifle. While few guerrilla organizations can aspire to the ownership of what may be regarded as any standard 'service' rifle, they will still use some form of rifle for combat. Exactly what that rifle might be depends on what can be obtained via the usual supply chains. A few general pointers as to the nature of the rifles involved can be detected, but before that a little consideration must be given to the shotgun.

Shotguns

The shotgun is undergoing something of a resurgence, in military terms. Although largely neglected as a military weapon until the First World War, it is now attracting a great deal of attention again and the weapon is once more finding its way into the established armouries. That is nothing new for guerrillas, for they have been using shotguns for decades.

Shotguns have been used by guerrillas for two main reasons. One is that the shotgun and its ammunition are fairly easy to obtain, and the second is that it is a devastating weapon at close ranges.

The majority of guerrilla shotguns come from civilian sources. In many nations the shotgun is widely used for hunting and sporting purposes, and is thus one of the first weapons a newly-converted guerrilla will take from the rack over his mantlepiece – the Cypriot EOKA movement of 1954-59 provides a good example of this form of taking up arms. Although the sporting shotgun has its limitations as a military weapon, it is better than nothing, even using sporting cartridge loads, and can be used in the usual process of obtaining something better. Once in guerrilla service the sporting shotgun be it the time-honoured single- or double-barrel type, or the more modern automatic (or 'pump') shotgun, is often modified in several ways.

One of the most common practices is the cutting back of the shotgun barrel(s) to a much shorter length. This has two advantages: one is that the weapon becomes easier to conceal, and the other is that it enables the shot fired to fan out in a much wider

Rifles and Shotguns 49

cone. The trouble with that modification is that the range can also be affected and will become even shorter than it was originally. The second alteration made is to the butt. This is frequently cut back and reshaped, again to reduce the length and make it easier to conceal. Shotguns altered in this style are often referred to as 'whipit' guns, and they are used wherever guerrillas operate.

The second reason for using shotguns, in modified or unmodified form, is that at short ranges they are dreadful weapons, capable of inflicting terrible wounds. They also require very little accurate aiming, especially when the barrels have been attenuated. Shot cartridge loads are meant to form a cone pattern as they leave the muzzle and thus really accurate aim is not required, which is just as well if the weapon is in the hands of barely-trained personnel. They are ideal anti-ambush weapons. In any ambush situations all that is required as the shooting starts is the pointing of the shotgun in a general direction and pulling the trigger. The shotgun does the rest and an attacker would be lucky to escape the lethal cone of shot at close ranges. The same attributes make the shotgun an ideal weapon in jungles or in certain urban warfare situations where combat ranges are short and where the shotgun can cover a large area with potentially dangerous projectiles.

The main drawback to the shotgun is its extremely short combat range. Most 12-bore shotguns are militarily ineffective at ranges of 40 metres or more, although a lucky hit could be wounding to a target. Some of the range drawbacks can be overcome by the use of solid projectiles (or 'slugs') in place of shot, but the range increases are only marginal. However, solid slugs fired from shotguns can be extremely harmful weapons. The 12-bore shotgun has a calibre of slightly less than 20 mm. Compare that to a rifle bullet of, say, 7.62 mm calibre and it can be imagined what the effect of a shotgun slug at close range could be. Shotgun slugs have the capability to penetrate sheet steel or timber baulks, but again, only at close range.

Virtually any shotgun can be used as a guerrilla weapon, but recent years have seen a number of 'new technology' designs appear on the scene. Most are intended specifically for the military or paramilitary market. Some of these weapons are beefed-up sporting shotguns, but among them are a few weapons with a large magazine capacity and the capability for semi-automatic or even fully automatic fire.

Among them is the Italian Franchi SPAS 12, a weapon that has caused much worry to police and other security forces. This shotgun has the ability to fire metal-piercing shot at high cyclic rates of fire, and has been designed from the outset with the harsh requirements of military employment in mind. It is a large rugged weapon and can be used to fire grenades from a muzzle launcher. The Franchi PA3, a pump action stablemate, is much smaller and handier. Both have now been joined by the Franchi SPAS 15, which has a 6-round box magazine and can be used as a semi-automatic or pump action weapon.

The thought of such weapons in the hands of guerrillas will make even the most experienced security operative apprehensive. Weapons such as the SPAS 12 can be purchased openly in many commercial markets, and some have already been used by criminals. It cannot be long before these or similar weapons end up in guerrillas hands.

As the basic shotgun is a simple weapon, in design terms, it is not all that difficult to produce in back street workshops. All that is required is a length of metal pipe of suitable strength and length, a rudimentary breech closing device and some form of trigger and striker mechanism. In the last resort the latter could be a nail struck by a stone. Such weapons have been made and used, and although they are virtually 'one shot' weapons, that shot has often proved to be too much for the unfortunate target concerned.

For some reason the Philippines have for many years been one of the main centres of improvised shotgun manufacture, some of them incorporating components from old shotguns or rifles and others produced to a surprisingly high standard. However, the main run of Philippine home-made shotguns are horrible-looking things that appear to be every bit as lethal to the user as to their intended target. The same can be said of most home-made shotguns produced elsewhere, especially the dreadfully crude shotguns produced by the Kenyan Mau-Mau between 1951 and 1955.

Rifles ~ general

Guerrilla forces have to use whatever weapons they can obtain, and that applies to rifles as well as other types of weapon.

However, during the last two decades two particular types of rifle have emerged as the standard weapons, without which no guerrillas can feel fully equipped. Before we consider those two types, a few general topics need examination.

After the Second World War there was no shortage of rifles almost anywhere in the world. During the war huge numbers of weapons, including rifles, were handed out to resistance and other guerrilla groups all over Europe and the Far East; very few were ever handed back to the original donors after 1945. Wherever battles were fought, weapons of all kinds, including rifles, were left on the battlefield, simply waiting to be picked up. Many *were* picked up and spirited away to await some possible future use. In the aftermath of the war, in many countries, nationalist or political organizations arose to use force to drive home their particular message. Thus any study of guerrilla movements from 1945 to the mid-1960s will soon reveal an array of the service weapons originally used by Second World War combatants. Included will be old Lee-Enfields, Mausers of all kinds, and American Springfield rifles. Italian rifles were also widespread and Japanese and American rifles proliferated throughout the Far East. By contrast, ex-Soviet weapons were few and far between, other than in Eastern Europe, and even there they did not last long in potentially dangerous hands. But many of these veterans still continue to crop up from time to time.

Unfortunately for the guerrillas using such rifles, the weapons involved had often seen hard use before they fell into their hands, and were often worn out and unreliable. The only thing to do at that time was either obtain reconditioned weapons or else purchase the cloned examples produced in locations such as the Pakistan-Afghanistan border areas. There, local craftsmen can still turn out close and serviceable copies of Lee-Enfields or other rifles, correct down to serial numbers and other detail.

For many guerrilla movements there was no need to use the usual theft or purchase methods of obtaining new weapons. The major powers soon observed the increasing importance of the guerrilla movements springing up all around the world, and began a process of handing out weapons of all kinds to the movements sympathetic to what they thought were their own aims. The first such hand-outs provided during the 1950s were usually yet more of the old Second World War relics. Gradually

that changed, and guerrilla movements began to receive brand
new weapons.

Since the Soviet Union and other Warsaw Pact nations felt inclined to provide more hand-outs than their American counterparts, more and more new Soviet weapons began to reach
guerrilla hands in sensitive areas such as the Middle and Far
East, Africa, and Central and South America.

Many of the post-1960 Soviet hand-outs included large
numbers of weapons such as the semi-automatic SKS, which was
a considerable improvement over the old bolt-action rifles. Then
numbers of AK-47 rifles began to appear, and before too long
the AK-47 became a virtual symbol of guerrilla movements all
over the world.

Today the AK-47, and its numerous derivatives and variations, is *the* guerrilla weapon. There is only one other weapon
that can even remotely approach it in numbers or popularity,
and that is the American M16A1 and its derivatives and
variants, generally known as the Armalites. But the AK-47 (and
the AKM) outnumber the Armalites by far.

The Kalashnikovs

The AK-47 can lay claim to having been produced in larger
numbers than any other rifle. Although accurate figures are impossible to come by, it seems likely that well over 12 million have
been produced, and as the type is still in production those
numbers are continually rising.

The AK-47 was developed following combat experience gained during the Second World War. German combat analysis in-
dicated that most infantry combats took place at ranges of less
than 400 metres, yet soldiers were equipped with weapons and
ammunition designed to give their best at ranges of up to 1,000
metres or more. The Germans accordingly designed less powerful ammunition (the 7.92 mm *kurz patrone* round) and weapons
to fire it from. The latter included the series of rifles based on the
Sturmgewehr 43, which were able to produce fully automatic fire
and thus produce far more firepower in action. The Red Army
took note of these developments and started their own investiga-
tions along similar lines.

Without going into too much development detail, the result
was a new Soviet 7.62 x 39 mm cartridge and a new rifle, the

AK-47, popularly known as the 'Kalashnikov' after the head of the design bureau involved, Mikhail Timofeyevich Kalashnikov. The AK-47 is what is now known as an assault rifle. It can fire its relatively low-powered ammunition (low powered compared to conventional rifle ammunition) either on single shot or fully automatic fire to a maximum effective combat range of around 400 metres. The ammunition is lethal beyond that range, but its ballistic performance is inclined to be erratic. Even so, the sights on the AK-47 are optimistically calibrated up to 800 metres (1,000 metres on the AKM).

The result is to provide the ordinary foot soldier with enhanced fire power at combat ranges. Trained soldiers can produce deliberate aimed fire using the single-shot fire mode, and switch to fully automatic for the assault or for close range combat. Untrained soldiers (and many guerrillas) tend to use their AK-47s on fully automatic all the time. The usual result is a waste of ammunition.

The AK-47 is a gas-operated weapon. As a round is fired, some of the propellant gas is tapped off from the barrel and used to activate an internal piston to operate all the case ejection, feed and cocking mechanisms. The system is simple and uses a minimum of components. Ammunition is fed into the weapon from a curved box magazine holding 30 rounds. Everything relating to the AK-47 is simple and rugged, to the point where it can seemingly absorb all manner of rough treatment and neglect and yet still keep on firing. Field stripping and maintenance is straightforward and involves only a few moving parts. Needless to say, the AK-47 is ideally suited to guerrilla operations.

The first production AK-47s were produced using machined components, including the main body of the weapon, the receiver. The butt stock was usually a simple wooden component, as was the pistol grip, but some AK-47s, intended originally for use by airborne forces, were fitted with a folding metal frame butt stock to save space when travelling or for stowage. Several other changes were introduced on the production lines during the AK-47's production life, but they were minor.

The original AK-47 was replaced in production during the late 1950s by a new variant that introduced the manufacturing expedient of using stampings and riveting for many components, in place of the earlier more expensive and time-consuming machining from solid metal. This version is known as the AKM, and

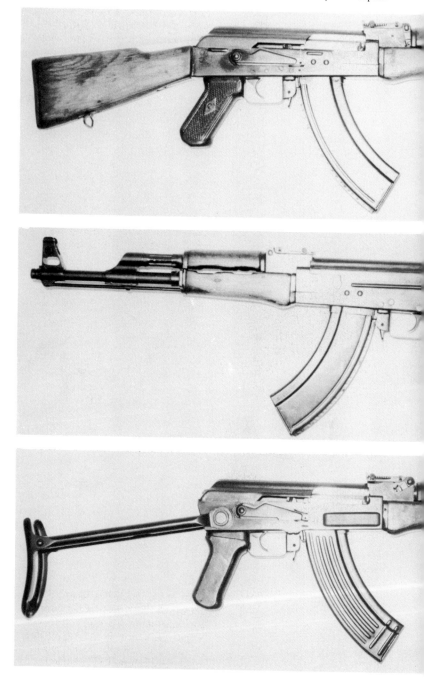

Left *An example from the very first Soviet AK-47 production batch. This had a machined receiver and two rivets, clearly seen here, above the point where the magazine enters the receiver* (T. Gander).

Left *Left-hand side of an early production Soviet AK-47* (T. Gander).

Left *A later production Soviet AK-47 without the twin rivets of the original production model but with a long rectangular depression in the side of the receiver. This example has the folding metal frame butt stock* (T. Gander).

although it differs from the earlier AK-47 in many respects, it is identical in operation, to the point where to the ordinary soldier the AKM is little different from the AK-47 (although the AKM is lighter). The easiest way of telling the AKM and the AK-47 apart is that the AKM has a prominent 'dimple' above the point where the magazine enters the receiver. There are many other detail differences that can be detected by close examination of the two rifles.

The AKM gradually replaced the earlier AK-47 in Soviet armed forces use, and as they were withdrawn the AK-47s were passed over to local militias and, eventually, guerrilla organizations. Huge numbers of the orginal AK-47s can still be found in guerrilla hands all around the world, but over the years they have been supplemented by equally large numbers of AKMs for the AKM has, in its turn, been replaced in Soviet front-line service by a new weapon, the AK-74, which is basically an AKM modified to fire a new and smaller 5.45 x 39 mm cartridge.

However, it will be many years before the AKM passes from large-scale Soviet use, and as yet it has not been mentioned that the AK-47 and AKM have been produced in huge numbers by nearly all the Warsaw Pact nations. By using its considerable political and economic clout, the Soviet Union has been able to impose a policy of strict equipment standardization on its Warsaw Pact allies, to the point where Soviet weapons are used to a large extent by almost all Eastern Bloc nations. Nearly all Warsaw Pact nations have produced their own AK-47 and AKM rifles. However, many have taken the opportunity to introduce their own local modifications to suit their production methods or to suit their own requirements. The result has been a seemingly bewildering array of AK-47 and AKM variants, increased further by the production of AK-47 and AKM variants by nations such as China, North Korea and Yugoslavia. Yet more variants have appeared on the scene from nations that have used the AK-47 or AKM as a design basis to produce what at first appear to be entirely different weapons. This has given rise to weapon designs such as the Israeli Galil (and from that the South African R-4) and the Finnish Valmet M60 series of assault rifles.

One assault rifle that appears to be an AK-47 variant but is not, is the Czech vzor 58. Despite its appearance, the internal workings of the vzor 58 have little to do with the AK-47. However, since the vzor 58 is also used by many guerrilla groups,

A Soviet-produced AKM. Note the pronounced dimple at the point where the magazine meets the receiver (T. Gander).

Soviet AKM complete with sling. The lever over the trigger and on the side of the receiver is the fire control change lever (T. Gander).

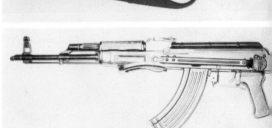

Soviet AKMS with butt folded (T. Gander).

Soviet AKMS with butt extended (T. Gander).

A Romanian AK-47, identifiable only by its markings (T. Gander).

A Polish AK-47 with folding metal butt stock (T. Gander).

The East German MPiKM is easily identified by the distinctive plastic butt. The similar MPiKMS-72 has a very simple folding wire butt stock and is issued by airborne troops (T. Gander).

Romanian-produced AKMs are easily identified by the wooden fore grip. Numbers of these weapons have appeared in Northern Ireland (T. Gander).

The Yugoslav M70 is based on the AKM but has a fixed grenade launcher fitted to the muzzle. The later M70B1 and M70AB2 lack the muzzle launcher but retain the overall high standard of finish (T. Gander).

The Czech Vzor 58 P uses a different operating mechanism. It is easily recognised by its different general outline and the use of compressed wood-fibre filled plastic furniture (T. Gander).

The Hungarian AMD-65 is one of the most easily identified of the AKM variants as it has been extensively redesigned. Note the new pistol and fore grips, the simple folding butt stock, the revised muzzle attachment and the revised fore stock. There are various other detail differences (T. Gander).

Hungarian AMD-65 with butt extended (T. Gander).

Right *A Chinese Type 56, unfortunately without its usual fixed bayonet which folds back under the barrel. This version is based on the AK-47 (T. Gander).*

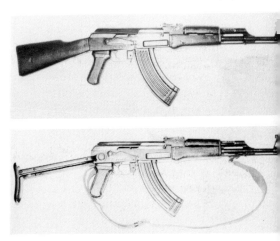

Right *A Chinese Type 56-1 with the folding metal frame butt stock. This version is based on the AK-47. In common with some other Type 56-1s, it does not have a bayonet (T. Gander).*

it is included here to complete the overall picture and provide a recognition guide.

Full details of the main differences between all these AK-47 and AKM variants are provided in the illustration captions that accompany this section. However, a few variants can fairly safely be eliminated from the list of weapons likely to be encountered in guerrilla hands. One is the Finnish Valmet rifle, few of these weapons have appeared outside Finland, despite a prolonged sales campaign, and to date production has been for the Finnish armed forces only. It is possible that numbers of Israeli Galil rifles have fallen into guerrilla hands, but the numbers involved must be small, almost as small as the numbers of captured or 'lost' South African R-4s (even the Angolan UNITA guerrillas use AK-47s). However, numbers of the more recent AK-74 (and its folding butt variant, the AKS-74) have been captured and used by Afghan Mujahadeen.

Of the huge number that remain, there are two main design variants. It has been mentioned that AK-47s can be found with either solid wood or folding metal frame butt stocks. The AKM is produced in the same two forms, but the wooden butt version is known simply as the AKM, while the metal butt version is the AKMS.

Detail design features of the AKM are a simple muzzle compensator, which is set at an angle to reduce muzzle jump on firing, and an ingenious bayonet and scabbard which can be combined to form a set of wire cutters. A basic cleaning and maintenance tool kit can be carried under the butt plate, and a shoulder sling can be fitted.

Perhaps the most widely-encountered of the non-Soviet AK-47 and AKM variants are the Chinese copies. The basic AK-47 Chinese copy is known as the Type 56, but the same designation was also used for a Chinese copy of the AKM. The main identification point for these weapons, apart from the Chinese character markings on the receiver, is the inclusion of an integral spike bayonet that folds back under the barrel. The Type 56-1 has a folding metal frame butt, while the later Type 56-2 introduced an unusual side-folding butt stock. Some Type 56-1 models do not have the fixed bayonet, and neither does the Type 56-2.

Many guerrilla organizations have become so well equipped with AK-47s and AKMs that the weapon has become a virtual standard. So widespread is their use that the very sight of any AK-47 or AKM, in any of its forms, virtually identifies the user as a guerrilla. More and more Kalashnikovs appear on the scene every year, and it seems that the AK-47 and AKM will be with us for decades to come.

Kalashnikov users have few problems with ammunition supply. Even ammunition manufacturers from Western nations now find it well worth their while to produce 7.62 x 39 mm ammunition. Types of ammunition likely to be encountered include ball, tracer, incendiary, blank and armour-piercing rounds. Most rifle users fire ball only.

Model	AK-47	AKM
Calibre	7.62 mm	7.62 mm
Weight	4.3 kg	3.15 kg
Length	869 mm	876 mm
Length of barrel	414 mm	414 mm
Magazine	30-round box	30-round box
Rate of fire (cyclic)	600 rpm	600 rpm
Muzzle velocity	710 m/s	710 m/s

The Armalites

The only rifle that can compare in numbers to the Kalashnikov series of rifles is the American rifle generally referred to as the Armalite. Despite the millions of Armalites that have been

Above *The 7.62 mm M14 was the standard American service rifle prior to the introduction of the M16 series. It was, and still is, a bulky and heavy weapon; this is the M16A1, the squad support weapon variant* (T. Gander).

Below *The Armalite 7.62 mm AR-10, the design that was the starting point for the M16* (T. Gander).

produced over the last few decades, the early weapons had a difficult time during the early stages of their development.

The term 'Armalite' does not refer to a single type of weapon, but rather to a series, originally produced by a concern now known as the ArmaLite Corporation Inc. This corporation was originally the ArmaLite Division of the Fairchild Engine and Aircraft corporation. During the early 1950s the concern was joined by one of the most prolific and successful small arms designers of the twentieth century, namely Eugene M. Stoner. It was not long after his arrival before ArmaLite were producing innovative weapon designs.

An early example of the novel approach used by ArmaLite was their AR-5. This is a small bolt-action .22 survival rifle, on which all the major components can be stripped down for stowage in the plastic butt stock. The US Air Force purchased a batch of these weapons, and the type is still available. Other weapon designs, including sporting shotguns, were produced. Then came the AR-10.

The AR-10 is one of small-arms history's many 'might-have-beens'. Despite its many innovative features, it arrived on the scene at a juncture where the American armed forces had just adopted the M14 rifle in place of the old M1 Garand. That changeover had already caused a great upheaval among the American military authorities, so when the AR-10 arrived it was not likely to have any real chance of adoption by the American armed forces, even though it was chambered to fire the then-novel 7.62 x 51 mm NATO standard ammunition.

The AR-10 operated very differently from anything that had gone before. Eugene Stoner used the AR-10 as the first venture incorporating his new rotary bolt-into-barrel lock involving multiple locking lugs and a two-part bolt. This locking system was gas-operated, positive and compact and allowed the incorporation of light alloys and other light materials in the general construction of the weapon. In fact the AR-10 locking and operation system proved to be so effective that it is now almost universally employed by many other weapon designs and types of weapon.

The AR-10 also looked very different from anything else. It employed the then rarely used all-in-line layout, with the barrel directly in a line with the butt - the sights were raised over the receiver in a housing that also acted as a carrying handle and shrouded the cocking lever. Ammunition was contained in a 20-round straight box magazine, forward of the trigger group. The muzzle was fitted with a large combined muzzle brake and flash hider. Overall, the appearance was futuristic and, for the time, extremely odd.

It was too odd for the American armed forces. They carried out a series of tests involving the weapon, but by that time the M14 was firmly established on the production lines and there was little chance of any changes being made to the armed force's procurement programmes, despite the M14 being far more bulky, complex and heavy than the AR-10.

The AR-10 was thus just too late. A few sales were made to countries such as the Sudan and Guatemala, but only a few. The basic design concept of the AR-10 was destined not to fade away, however. It was used again during the late 1950s, after a prolonged period of trials and experiments during which the American armed forces searched for something better than the then-current 7.62 x 51 mm NATO cartridge. The Americans had lumbered themselves (and other NATO armed forces) with this powerful cartridge, despite the findings of the many Second World War combat analysis teams who had thoroughly investigated many combat fire-fights to determine any possible trends or lessons. They, like the Germans before them, discovered that the vast majority of infantry fire-fights took place at ranges of well under 400 metres, yet the weapons involved fired ammunition that was designed to produce its best at ranges of 1,000 metres or more. The introduction of less powerful ammunition could permit the use not only of lighter infantry weapons, but also of weapons capable of fully automatic fire.

The American planners seized upon the notion of automatic rifles, but went against the concept of less powerful ammunition. They decided to replace their old .30-06 Springfield cartridge with the 7.62 x 51 cartridge, which was only marginally shorter than its predecessor (the case was 51 mm long compared to the earlier 63 mm) but was every bit as powerful as the earlier cartridge, thanks to the introduction of modern propellants. Powerful cartridges require strong and heavy weapons to fire them, so the US Army had to abandon a project known as the Lightweight Rifle Program, and ended up with the bulky and non-lightweight M14 rifle at a time when other nations were already moving towards lighter weapons. The AR-10 was but one advanced design in a general movement towards the use of modern technological innovations and materials.

Despite the seemingly inherent conservatism of the military, some American design agencies began to experiment with small calibre cartridges. There were many of these, some firing multiple projectiles, but one cartridge seemed to offer considerable promise. This emerged as the 5.56 x 45 mm high velocity (1,000 m/s) cartridge, that in time became the M193.

ArmaLite produced a rifle to fire the new 5.56 mm (0.22-inch) cartridge. The new rifle was virtually a scaled-down AR-10 and became known as the AR-15. From the start, the AR-15 was the subject of much controversy - in some ways it still is. The AR-15 carried over many of the design features of the earlier AR-10, but in a smaller scale. As a result it was constructed using light alloy castings, with nylon-based plastics for much of the weapon's furniture (butt and fore stocks and pistol grip). The all-in-line layout was retained, and so was the characteristic handle over the receiver to carry the rear sight. The cocking piece was moved to the back of the receiver.

The thoroughly modern appearance of the AR-15 initially mitigated against it as far as the American military were concerned. They had been brought up in a school where something as outlandish in appearance as the AR-15 did not fit into any service category. When combined with the novel small-calibre 5.56 x 45 mm ammunition, the very concept of the AR-15 seemed to place it in a toy class.

A series of demonstrations and trials gradually altered that outlook. The AR-15 proved to be a very effective weapon, despite its appearance. Gradually the weapon won service acceptance. Soldiers who had to carry the AR-15 liked its light weight and the general handiness of the weapon. This was particularly important after the Americans began their involvement in South-East Asia, and especially Vietnam. It was noted that the AR-15 was particularly suited to the small-statured peoples of the region, and it was also noted that American 'advisers' operating with the local armed forces favoured the AR-15 more than their M14s or other weapons.

Gradually the AR-15 was accepted by the American staff planners. It was even adopted for what was planned to be 'limited service' as the M16. By then production had switched from ArmaLite to the mighty Colt's Patent Firearms Manufacturing Company. Production totals were soaring and the 'limited service' approach was soon left far behind. Gradually the production totals entered the tens of thousands, then the hundreds of thousands and eventually the millions. Today the production total stands at well over 8,000,000 and the numbers are still rising.

It was combat experience in Vietnam that turned the tide. In that theatre the AR-15, by then the M16, proved to be a highly effective and popular weapon, even managing to survive a period where prolonged stoppages began to appear during combat (the cause was found to be an unannounced change in ammunition propellant type and a general lack of proper maintenance). Training soon removed the latter cause, and the introduction of

GUERRILLA FIREPOWER

Above *Although large and heavy, the 7.62 mm SG43 machine-gun is still used by many guerrilla groups for its fire power effects on all manner of targets.*

Below *The SA-7 'Grail' surface-to-air missile (top), with its launcher beneath.*

Above The Soviet 7.62 mm PKM
machine-gun, originally intended to be a
general purpose machine-gun, but used
for all manner of roles by guerrillas in
many parts of the world.

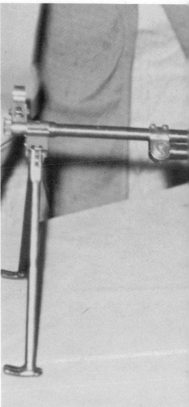

Above right The Soviet PPSh sub-
machine-gun, produced in millions during the Second World War and still used
by many guerrilla groups. This weapon is
often encountered with a drum magazine
fitted in place of the curved box shown
here.

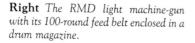

Right The RMD light machine-gun
with its 100-round feed belt enclosed in a
drum magazine.

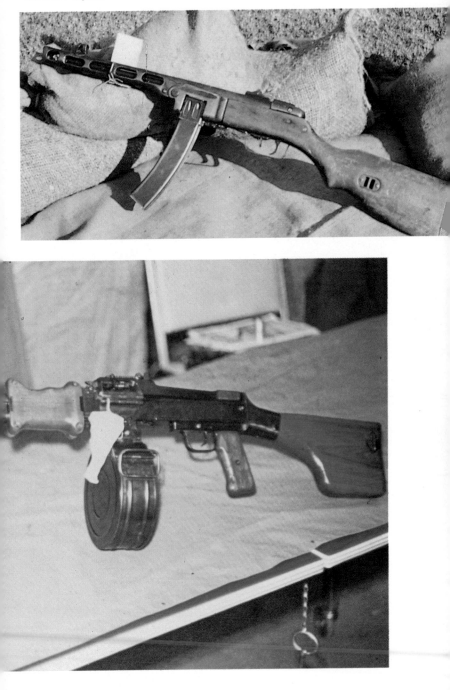

Above *The AK-47, the virtual badge of the modern guerrilla.*

Right *The Soviet RPG-7, intended to be an anti-tank rocket launcher but used by guerrillas as a close range support or strike weapon against all manner of targets.*

Below *The bayonet used with the AK-47 and AKM, which can be readily converted into handy wire-cutters.*

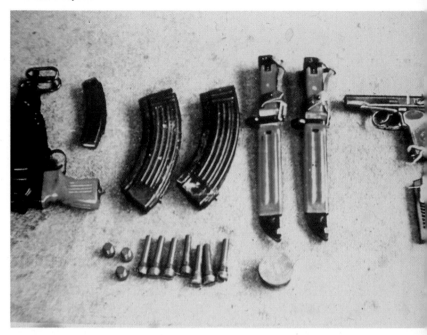

Above *A typical security force find in the constant round of searches: from left, a Skorpion machine-pistol, AKM magazines, two AK-47/AKM bayonets, a PM pistol and detonators.*

Below *A limpet mine, often used by guerrillas to terrible effect against urban targets.*

Above 60 mm mortar bombs, used by guerrillas not only for launching from their intended light mortars, but also adapted for use in booby traps and as land mines.

Above Left Items to watch out for: a few of the items used to activate and prepare limpet mines for use.

Left The contents of a typical car bomb; thankfully this one was de-activated before it could be set off.

Above A mine activation switch used by guerrillas operating during their prolonged campaign in Rhodesia.

Below This innocuous-looking substance is Semtex, a Czech plastic explosive widely used by guerrillas due to its extreme power.

a bolt closure device removed the chances of similar stoppages occurring in the future. The modification was introduced on the M16A1, which has been the most-produced AR-15 variant to date.

Production of the AR-15/M16 was carried out not only in the United States but in Singapore, South Korea and the Philippines. Not only did numbers of AR-15/M16 derivatives appear but some nations used the AR-15/M16 as a basis for their own weapon designs. The 5.56 mm Type 65 rifle produced in Taiwan uses many M16 components and is largely made using M16 production machine tools. The Communist Chinese have produced a M16 clone, known as the 5.56 mm Type 311 (originally known as the Type CQ), apparently for the export market only.

With so many M16s in service, it became inevitable that some were to end up in guerrilla hands. Needless to say, South-East Asia was a prime source of supply. During the Vietnam conflict many M16s were freely handed out by the Americans to various local forces, both regular and irregular. Few efforts were made to monitor how and when those weapons were used or deployed, and many eventually passed into guerrilla hands. More were more or less openly sold to guerrillas by conniving local regular armed forces recipients. The totals involved were increased when the Americans finally left Vietnam. Behind them they left huge stockpiles of M16s (and many other weapons) and their ammunition, and even larger numbers of M16s that had been 'lost on the battlefield' or which had otherwise gone adrift. Yet more M16s that had been issued to the South Vietnamese armed forces ended up with various forms of guerrilla organizations.

In many ways the AR-15/M16 is an ideal guerrilla weapon. It is light, handy and relatively small and it is easy to handle and fire. The 5.56 x 45 mm ammunition produces little in the way of recoil forces, even when fired in the fully automatic mode, so initial acceptance by untrained recruits is easy - even children can fire the AR-15/M16 without any problem. During the Vietnam conflict the M16 proved to be excellent for the form of jungle warfare often involved. Guerrillas operating in similar terrain can also have few of the problems they encounter using larger weapons. Ammunition supply is rarely a problem since 5.56 x 45 mm ammunition is widely available - it is even produced in Communist China (although this differs in several respects from M193 standards).

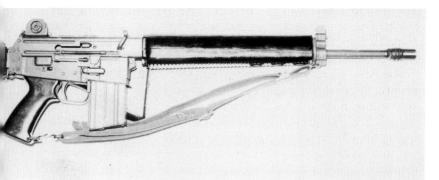

Above *The 5.56 mm Armalite AR-18, a design that owed little to earlier models and which is now widely used by guerrilla organizations, including the IRA. This example has its side-folding butt stowed in the closed position* (T. Gander).

Below *The AR-18S was a carbine version of the AR-18 that was supposed to convert the AR-18 into a form of sub-machine gun. Few were produced* (T. Gander).

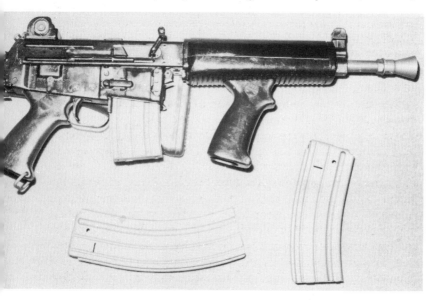

The AR-15/M16 is not the only form of rifle referred to as an Armalite. After Eugene Stoner left ArmaLite, they produced a new design known as the ArmaLite AR-18. Compared to the earlier AR-15 the AR-18 is slightly smaller, uses a different operating mechanism and makes use of sheet metal stampings in place of light alloy castings. Some versions use a side-folding butt stock. The objective was to produce a low cost weapon that could be manufactured more easily than the AR-15. To date, the AR-18 has been less of a sales success than the earlier design.

The AR-18 has been licence-produced in various countries, including the United Kingdom, but as far as is known, none have been adopted by any regular armed force. Some have been sold to police forces and other paramilitary security forces, while others have been sold to commercial organizations that turned out to be nothing more than 'fronts' for guerrilla arms procurement. In its turn, the AR-18 has given rise to a number of other weapons using the same design basis - the Singapore-produced SAR 80 assault rifle is but one example.

Thus the AR-18 is now widely used by several guerrilla organizations throughout the world, and is one of the IRA's more favoured weapons, to the extent that they have announced their political policy of 'the ballot box and the Armalite'. The latter must be one of the few examples of a political message involving the name of a weapon. (Another well-known example can be found in the old Irish Rebel song 'In the Green', where mention is made of '...the rattle of a Thompson Gun'.)

The Armalites are not just one series of weapons but several, all light and handy weapons that can prove to be highly effective in the right hands. So many are now in guerrilla hands that they now act as the only rival to the AK-47 and AKM as a symbol of guerrilla activity, and in some parts of the world the Armalite in its many forms is now a standard guerrilla weapon. Examples can be found in the Philippines, where locally-produced M16s are used by the Communist-inspired New People's Army, in Sri Lanka where several of the various Tamil groups have obtained large numbers of M16s, and in the Lebanon where many of the militia factions favour the M16 over the AK-47 or AKM, although carrying of the latter weapons is favoured by some militia groups.

A direct comparison of the various forms of Armalite and Kalashnikov rifles is not easy. They are totally different designs from different design backgrounds, but the general trend of opinion is that the laurels must go to the Kalashnikovs. Not only are they in use in far greater numbers than the Armalites, but they are judged to be more robust. Although the Armalites may be handier and lighter to carry, their use of light alloys and plastics makes them much more vulnerable to hard knocks and wear than their more solid Soviet rivals. The Kalashnikovs are also much more forgiving of lack of proper maintenance than the Armalites. To the trained soldier these two points may be of limited importance, but to the guerrilla they are extremely important.

Then there is the question of the ammunition involved. The projectile fired by the 7.62 x 39 mm cartridge is heavier and potentially much more harmful than its 5.56 x 45 mm equivalent, but set against that the smaller calibre bullet can produce dreadful wounds under certain circumstances. However, as has already been mentioned, the 5.56 mm calibre is still the subject of much controversy, much of it coming from front-line troops who have fired 5.56 mm ammunition in combat. Many troops have appreciated the on-target effectiveness of the high velocity small calibre ammunition, but have noted that it often seems to lack stopping power at longer ranges. They have also asked for cartridges that produce more 'punch'. By contrast, few complaints seem to come from troops (or guerrillas) using the Soviet 7.62 mm ammunition.

Some of the complaints regarding 5.56 mm ammunition may be met by the adoption of a new NATO standard 5.56 x 45 mm cartridge based on the Belgian SS109 design. The M16A2 has been developed and issued to the US Army and Marine Corps to fire this new round. Even the Soviet armed forces have followed the trend to smaller calibres, by their adoption of a new 5.45 x 39 mm cartridge for firing from the AK-74 series of assault rifles. The small size of the Soviet bullet is partially overcome ballistically by the use of a steel core (also used by the 5.56 mm SS 109) and a soft nose that is designed to buckle as it strikes a target and make the bullet 'tumble' to produce larger wounds.

Eventually both of these new types of ammunition and weapons to fire them will end up in guerrilla hands, and no doubt they will be happy to use either.

Model	M16A1	AR-18
Calibre	5.56 mm	5.56 mm
Weight	3.18 kg	3.17 kg
Length	990 mm	940 mm
Length of barrel	508 mm	464 mm
Magazine	20 or 30 rounds	20, 30 or 40 rounds
Muzzle velocity	1000 m/s	1000 m/s
Cyclic rate of fire	750-900 rpm	850 rpm

Other rifles

With the Kalashnikovs and the Armalites covered, the other guerrilla rifles can be more briefly mentioned. The easiest way to cover the topic is simply to say that anything goes, for guerrillas will use whatever rifles they can obtain. Having said that, there are a few rifle types that seem to crop up more than most.

The first group to be mentioned is the old Second World War residue, still making the rounds of the international arms business. Many guerrilla organizations have little recourse but to purchase what weapons are available, and as every shady arms dealer seems to have a stock of Second World War relics, they are often the cheapest and easiest weapons to purchase. There are four main weapon types in this category.

First come the old Lee-Enfield rifles. Some of these are not so old, for production of the 0.303 No.4 Mark 1 did not cease in the United Kingdom until the 1950s. The more venerable No.1 Mark III, used during the First World War, remained in production in

Below *The Lee-Enfield No 4 Mark I was meant to replace the old No 1 Mark III, but both types still soldier on together (T. Gander).*

Bottom *One military veteran that is still widely encountered is the Lee-Enfield No 1 Mark III. Originally produced prior to the First World War, this superb 0.303 rifle is still manufactured in workshops along the North-West Frontier between Pakistan and Afghanistan.*

India until only a few years ago, while the same rifle was produced in Australia until 1957. Craftsmen along the old North-West
Frontier are still turning out Lee-Enfield copies. Thus not all Lee-
Enfields on offer are likely to be ancient, and small numbers may
be encountered rebored to take 7.62 x 51 mm NATO ammunition. However, the weapons guerrillas are likely to get will be well
worn and of uncertain age or provenance. But old Lee-Enfields
can still be very serviceable weapons. Even war-time manufactured
Lee-Enfields were well made, using the best material available. As
long as there is ammunition for them to fire (reliable 0.303 ammunition is now becoming increasingly scarce ~ new ammunition
remains in production only in nations such as India, South Africa
and Greece) the Lee-Enfield rifles will remain serviceable weapons.

Then there are the Mausers. Until 1945 Mauser rifles were in
service all around the world. Many were local licence-produced
examples in any number of calibres, but in Europe the main cartridge used was the 7.92 x 57 mm, the standard service cartridge
of the old German Army. In the aftermath of 1945, virtually all
these ex-German rifles, and many more besides, were gathered up
and either scrapped or stockpiled. The stockpiles gradually fell into
the hands of the dealers, and many therefore ended up in some
very odd places. The bulk of these old Mausers were the Model
98k, the standard rifle of the German armed forces of 1939~45
but there were many other variants. These veterans still crop up
from time to time in the Middle East, South America and
elsewhere. Some of them will be found rebarrelled to take 7.62 x
51 mm NATO ammunition ~ these will be found to be nearly all
from ex-Israeli stocks, since the Israelis used many ex-German
Mausers during the early years of their national existence. As with
other rifle designs of their era, the Mausers were well made from
the finest materials, although some late war period Mausers are
very poor by comparison with earlier examples.

American Springfield rifles (the M1903 series) can still be found
in guerrilla use, especially in the Far East where many were freely
handed out to local populations for village defence and other purposes, as late as the Vietnam war period. Relatively few M1
Garands seem to have followed the same path and today few M1s
appear to be in guerrilla use. By contrast, the later M14 rifle keeps
turning up in guerrilla-infested locations such as the Philippines,
South-East Asia and the Horn of Africa.

The nearest Soviet equivalent to these old Second World War

The German 7.92 mm Kar 98k is typical of the many old Mauser rifles that are still in use all around the world. This example dates from 1935-45 (T. Gander).

Still in use in South-East Asia is the American .30 M1903 Springfield rifle.

An oddity in design terms, many millions of the American M1 were produced before 1945. The M1 fires a unique 0.30 cartridge which has proved to be under-powered.

The Soviet 7.62 mm Mosin-Nagant M1944, the last of a long line of Mosin-Nagant rifles that started back in 1895.

The Soviet 7.62 mm SKS was one of the first semi-automatic rifles produced in the Soviet Union after 1945.

The Belgian FAL was the starting point for many variations, but this 7.62 mm example is typical.

Typical of the many variants of the Heckler & Koch G-3 series of rifles is the 5.56 mm HK53 (T. Gander).

bolt-action rifles is the Mosin Nagant Model 1944 carbine firing
the 7.62 × 54 mm rimmed cartridge. This cut-down rifle was the
last major variant of the Mosin-Nagant rifle that dated back to
1895 and was produced in very large numbers during the latter
stages of the Second World War. Being short in length, easy to
handle and firing readily-available ammunition, the Model 1944
was widely distributed during the first period of Soviet support for
various guerrilla movements following 1945. The Soviets were no
doubt glad to be rid of their stocks, since almost as soon as the
Model 1944 entered service the first of the post-war Soviet-designed
semi-automatic rifles was ready for issue. This was the SKS, the
first weapon produced to fire the then-novel 7.62 x 39 mm short
cartridge. The SKS was one of the shorter-lived of the Soviet rifles,
so many were later relegated to military aid hand-out weapons,
and from there made their way into guerrilla use. Huge numbers
of the Model 1944 carbine and the SKS are still to be found in guerrilla hands all around the world, especially in Central and Southern
Africa.

The path followed by the SKS was also followed by many other
of the rifles produced from 1945 onwards. Of the numbers of types
likely to be encountered, two rifles from the later period seem to
prevail over all others. One is the Belgian 7.62 mm FAL (*Fusil
Automatique Legère* - light automatic rifle), one of the most successful of Belgian-post war weapon designs, and one sold and used throughout the world. It has been produced in the hundreds
of thousands and is still in licence production in some countries.
Being available in large numbers, it is not surprising that large
numbers have found their way into guerrilla hands. The British-
produced L1A1 rifle is a variant of the FAL but relatively few of
these seem to have entered large-scale guerrilla employment, other
than examples captured during local campaigns such as the operations against EOKA guerrillas in Cyprus from 1954-'59. As in
all such campaigns, not all captured weapons were recovered,
and some remained hidden or in the guerrilla weapons supply
network.

There is one relatively modern rifle that is in use by guerrillas
as disparate as the Kurds in Iraq and the IRA in Northern Ireland.
This the the Heckler & Koch G-3, a West German rifle that was
designed from the outset with ease of production as one of its main
features. The G-3 became the standard rifle of the Bundeswehr
from 1959 onwards, and since then it has been licence-produced

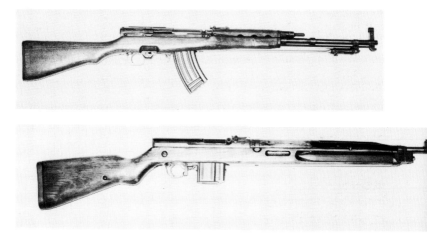

Top *The Chinese 7.62 mm Type 68 is an odd weapon that embodies features of both the Soviet AK-47 and the earlier SKS (T. Gander).*

Above *The 7.62 mm Model M52/57 features a folding bayonet and fires the Czech 7.62 × 45 mm cartridge. It has been encountered in guerrilla hands in certain parts of Africa.*

in many countries including Greece, Mexico, the Philippines, Burma and Iran.

The latter nation should be seen as the most important of these producers in guerrilla terms, for the G-3 was the standard service rifle of the old Imperial Iranian armed forces. Following the fall of the Shah, huge numbers of G-3s were freely distributed to 'revolutionary guards'. From such untrained and often careless hands, G-3s found their way to the underground arms supply market or were passed on to sympathetic guerrilla movements, notably the Kurds.

But Iran is not responsible for all the G-3s that are now relatively freely available. The list of user nations is a very long one indeed, including no fewer than 15 African nations. In some of these user nations there is always the chance that service rifles will go 'missing' or will be sold to customers with the right price in cash or kind. Consequently G-3s are used by guerrillas in considerable numbers.

The G-3 has been produced in a variety of models. Most guerrilla examples will be found chambered for the 7.62 x 51 mm NATO cartridge, with later models firing 5.56 x 45 mm. Some have orthodox butt stocks, while others use a telescoping form of metal stock. They all use the same roller locking delayed blowback operating principle, which has proved to be positive, safe and extremely reliable under all conditions. The layout of the weapon is conventional and much use is made of sheet metal pressings and plastics in the construction.

The list of possible guerrilla rifles could continue indefinitely, but we have covered the main types. The only item remaining to be mentioned is that every year more and more Chinese-produced rifles turn up in guerrilla hands. The vast majority of these are Kalashnikov copies, but of late the Chinese have taken to producing the already-mentioned M16 clone (the Type 311, or Type CQ) and have even seen fit to copy the American M14. They are also producing weapons such as their Type 68, a sort of cross between the Soviet SKS and the AK-47.

It will be noted that no mention has been made of sniper rifles. This omission has been deliberate, for although some trained guerrillas like to use sniper rifles to 'take out' selected targets or otherwise create long-range havoc, such weapons are not widely used by the usual run of guerrilla. Not only do sniper rifles need care and attention to use properly, but they also take a great deal of looking after. Under most operational conditions encountered by guerrillas, such care is rarely possible. Without careful handling, maintenance and calibration, sniper rifles soon become nothing more than expensive examples of useless military hardware.

PISTOLS AND SUB-MACHINE GUNS

The pistol and the sub-machine gun are listed here together for the reason that they both use the same type of ammunition, i.e. pistol ammunition. Apart from that, the two types of weapon have little in common, other than their supposed obsolescence, and will be dealt with separately.

Pistols

The pistol, in both its revolver and automatic form, has few obvious military uses today. However, it survives as a guerrilla weapon for the same reason that it survives in more regular military hands, i.e. there is nothing to replace it. It is small, light, portable, easy to conceal and, used properly, is lethal. It is also inherently unsafe unless carefully handled, and it has a very short combat range.

In guerrilla hands the pistol is primarily an assassination weapon. It is a weapon much used by urban guerrillas, often for purely terrorist purposes or for fund raising, i.e. criminal activities such as bank raids. The urban guerrilla rarely has the opportunity to carry any weapon larger than a pistol (other than an explosive device), so for him it is a pistol or nothing.

The rural guerrilla has little combat use for the pistol. It has far too short a combat range (not more than 20 metres in untrained hands, and often much less than that) but if a pistol is drawn or flourished, it does dictate compliance with orders. Thus many guerrilla leaders like to carry or display pistols as a symbol of authority, or to impress others.

But as mentioned above, the pistol is primarily a guerrilla assassination weapon. It can be carried concealed to a target, drawn and fired rapidly, and is just as easily hidden again. For this reason, silenced pistols are favoured by some guerrillas especially of the urban variety. This usually involves fitting some sort of silencer (or more accurately, sound moderator) device on to the muzzle of almost any type of pistol. However, a very few special assassination pistols with integral silencers have been produced for guerrilla and other undercover agent use.

One of the very first of these was the British Welrod pistol of the Second World War. Only a few of these were made, and were parachuted into Occupied Europe before the war ended, but they attracted a great deal of attention from potential guerrilla organizers. One result was the Chinese 7.65 mm Type 64 silenced pistol.

The Type 64 resembles an automatic pistol, but has a bulky integral silencer wrapped inside a casing around the barrel. To moderate the sound of firing further, the Type 64 fires a special 7.65 x 17 mm rimless low-powered cartridge that is used by no other weapon. The Type 64 can fire this ammunition using two fire modes. One mode is a purely single-shot pistol, in which the slide has to be hand-operated to remove a spent case and load a new round. By moving a selector bar, though, the pistol can operate as a normal automatic, but the moving slide will then produce more sound. The Type 64 was later joined by the essentially similar Type 67 pistol, also firing the same low-powered ammunition. The main change introduced to the Type 67 is that the silencer is contained in a more compact cylindrical housing around the short barrel.

Both the Type 64 and the Type 67 have appeared in guerrilla hands, mainly in the Far East, but the numbers involved have been small. Even fewer of a North Korean counterpart, also known as the Type 64, but having nothing to do with the Chinese weapon, have appeared. The North Korean 7.65 mm Type 64 is based on the old Browning Model 1900 and has a shortened slide to accommodate the bulk of a silencer tube over the end of the barrel. It fires conventional ammunition.

It is possible that a Second World War pistol concept might reappear in a modern form of the American 0.45 Liberator. This was a very small and simple pistol made from the cheapest-possible materials, mainly metal stampings, and intended for use against occupying forces by resistance fighters of various forms. The Liberator was meant to be dropped over occupied areas wrapped in plastic bags containing one pistol, a few 0.45 rounds and basic instructions presented in graphic 'comic strip' form. The design of the Liberator was so basic that once a round had been fired, the spent case had to be poked out using a short twig or a piece of wire. Needless to say it was a 'one shot' weapon, intended for use at the closest possible range. The Liberator design cropped up again during the Vietnam conflict when an

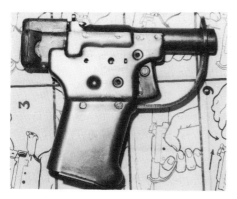

Left *A Liberator pistol, set against its instruction sheet and showing its simple and cheap construction* (T. Gander).

Below *The Soviet 7.62 mm TT-33, a pistol that can lay good claim to being produced in larger numbers than any other pistol.*

Below *A Soviet 7.62 mm Pistolet Makarova, now the standard pistol of the Soviet armed forces but one which is encountered increasingly frequently in guerrilla hands* (T. Gander).

essentially similar weapon known as the Deer Gun was devised, this time in 9mm. It was never issued.

The Liberator and Deer Gun are mentioned here, for it is always possible that something similar will be produced in the future for guerrillas, or even by them. The Liberator used only a few basic components that could be easily knocked out in garages or very basic workshops (the barrel was an unrifled steel tube) and assembled by unskilled hands. There is no reason why any well-organized guerrilla organization could not do the same. The end product would remain essentially an assassination weapon, but enough guerrillas armed with these simple pistols could wreak unimaginable terror in a crowd or on public transport.

The old adage that guerrillas will use any weapons that come their way remains true for pistols, only more so. There is no way an account of the pistols likely to be encountered in guerrilla hands can be provided here, other than a few very general pointers.

One pointer is that the old Soviet TT-33 automatic pistol is very widely used by guerrillas. The TT-33, also known as the Tokarev, went out of production in the Soviet Union during 1954, but as it had been in production since 1933 and throughout the war years, it seems very likely that it holds the record for being produced in larger numbers than any other automatic pistol ever made. It has been removed from Soviet armed forces front-line service, but is still used by reserve forces and militias.

The TT-33 is a simple and very robust weapon that fires the 7.62 x 25 mm cartridge used by several other Soviet weapons. The TT-33 is still in production in China (as the Type 54) and in Yugoslavia (as the Model M57). Almost any nation or organization that has received military aid from the Soviet Union will have received TT-33s in the process. Nations and organizations in the Far East will have received Type 54s from China, and Yugoslavia has offered the Model M57 on the export market.

Another widely-distributed pistol is the American Colt 0.45 M1911 or M1911A1, also known as the Colt 'Government' model. This large and relatively heavy pistol may be encountered wherever there has been American influence, and in a good many other places besides. The M1911 series has been manufac-

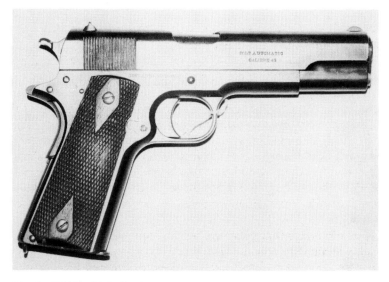

Above *'Old Faithful', the American 0.45 M1911A1.*

tured in numbers running into millions, and has been widely licence-produced or copied. Some nations such as Spain have

Below *A 0.455 Webley pistol, a heavy revolver that is still in guerrilla use in parts of Asia and Africa mainly due to the prodigious manstopping power of its bullet.*

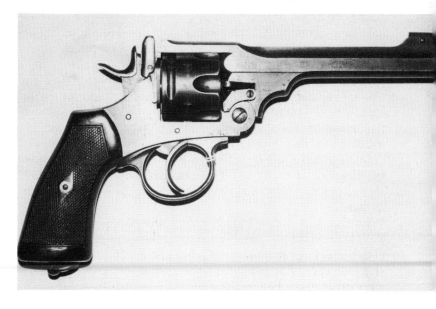

Right *A home-made pistol produced by converting an old flare pistol to accommodate a shotgun cartridge.*

Below *Another machine pistol, the Czech 7.62 mm Skorpion.*

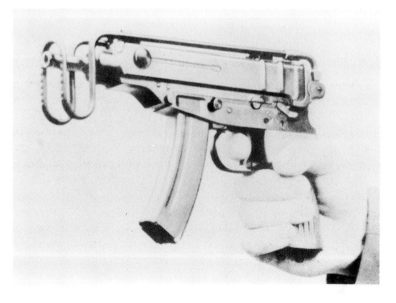

produced numerous pistol designs that are virtual clones of the M1911, and at one time the pistol was also copied in China and Argentina. The original M1911s were produced to fire a 0.45-inch bullet that was intended to be a certain 'man-stopper', after smaller pistol calibres proved to be ineffective against fanatical Moro guerrillas during the 1899–1902 American campaign to take over the Philippines. The 0.45 bullet is still a dreadfully effective projectile, but the M1911 is a bit of a handful to use properly and its muzzle blast and recoil forces make it a weapon to be respected by untrained users.

In India, Pakistan and places such as Burma, the old Webley revolver continues to turn up in its many forms. It may also be encountered in certain parts of Africa. Compared to other types of weapon, relatively few ex-Second World War German pistols crop up in use by guerrillas. Despite the large numbers that were either captured or appropriated as souvenirs during and after the war, pistols such as the Luger P '08 or Walther P 38 are now much sought-after collectors' items, and can command prices well in excess of what a guerrilla might be willing or able to pay.

Apart from those few very general pointers, almost anything in the pistol line is likely to be found in guerrilla hands, ranging from old revolvers dating back to the First World War, to shiny chrome-plated Smith & Wesson revolvers intended for the general commercial or police market.

Sub-machine guns

The sub-machine gun might have been designed specifically for the guerrilla. It is a simple weapon, capable of producing large amounts of fire, yet it is relatively light, easy to conceal and easy to look after. It does have the disadvantage of a rather short combat range (200 metres is usually regarded as the absolute maximum), but as most guerrilla combat takes place at well under that distance, that drawback matters little. Yet despite all its apparent advantages, the sub-machine gun is now little used by guerrillas. Exactly why requires a little study.

Although the sub-machine gun first appeared towards the end of the First World War, it did not make any particular impact until the Second World War. During that conflict the sub-machine gun soon became a widely-used weapon, and in some instances even replaced other weapon types in combat. The Soviet 'tank

Above *The Sten Mark 2, a typical example of how simple and cheap sub-machine guns can be produced. The Sten provided a starting point for a whole new aspect of the small-arms industry (T. Gander).*

descent' troops, who rode into action on the backs of tanks, carried nothing else, apart from grenades. As well as being an extremely useful combat weapon, the sub-machine gun also proved to be an economical one. It was soon discovered that actually manufacturing effective sub-machine guns made few demands on industry.

The classic example of the economy factor can be seen in the Sten Gun. Using the German MP 38 and MP 40 as production technique examples, the British were able to produce an effective sub-machine gun design that required little else other than steel tubing, metal stampings, a few springs and a handful of rivets. The end result looked dreadful, but it worked and was as lethal as far more expensive and conventionally-produced sub-machine guns. Few moving parts were involved, since the Sten used the blow-back locking principle in which the sheer forward inertia of a heavy breech block and a recoil spring 'locked' the weapon at the instant of firing. It took time for the recoil forces to overcome the inertia, and by then chamber pressures had fallen to safe levels.

The Sten was designed for front-line use, but it was also highly effective as a guerrilla weapon in the occupied territories of Europe. Huge numbers of Stens were delivered to the various resistance organizations in Europe, and the Sten proved to be ideal for their purposes. The weapon could be easily broken down into its main assemblies for concealment, it required little maintenance, and ammunition supply was relatively simple. The

Middle Left *The American 0.45 M3 sub-machine gun followed the same general cheap-and-cheerful production lines as the British Sten and it is still in the US Armed Forces inventory. Numbers have also found their way into guerrilla use in the Far East* (T. Gander).

Left *One Soviet equivalent of the Sten was the 7.62 mm PPSh-41, a weapon still widely encountered in guerrilla hands, especially in Africa* (T. Gander).

Sten fired the same 9 x 19mm Parabellum pistol ammunition used by the Germans.

The Sten also proved easy to copy and manufacture in underground workshops. All over Europe the clandestine production of Stens became a virtual industry. While the end products were frequently even more rough and ready than the original Stens, they still worked effectively enough. The only component that presented any problem to make was the magazine and its feed spring. Home-produced Stens used either proper Sten magazines or captured German items. Breechblocks could be turned out on simple machine tools, or even produced using hand tools only.

The example of the Sten is still there for guerrillas to follow. Wherever guerrillas have operated, from Northern Ireland to the Philippines, some form or other of home-made sub-machine gun has appeared. Many of these home-made weapons have, of course, blown up in use, but others have not.

The Sten Gun has now all but passed away. It is possible that a few are still used by guerrillas in odd corners of the world, but most guerrilla organizations can now aspire to something better.

That something better is almost always an assault rifle, in either its Armalite or Kalashnikov form. When the sub-machine gun was first introduced it was intended to be a hand-held weapon that could produce automatic fire. Since it was not possible to produce controlled automatic fire using the powerful rifle cartridges of the day, the only thing to do was to use low-

Below *In many ways the Thompson sub-machine gun was the prime guerrilla weapon and was a particular favourite of the IRA. Its day has now passed, but it still has a dramatic and distinctive appearance* (T. Gander).

powered pistol cartridges. They could produce automatic fire from a compact weapon that could be held under control, but the combat ranges were short, even when firing on single shot. When the assault rifle arrived on the scene during the Second World War, it virtually rendered the sub-machine gun obsolete. Firing as it does the intermediate-powered 'short' rifle cartridges, the assault rifle can deliver controllable automatic fire at ranges far in excess of those of the sub-machine gun. It can also deliver accurate single shots to useful combat ranges.

Thus as more and more assault rifles came into guerrilla use, the sub-machine gun declined in importance. But despite that decline, it has never vanished entirely. Almost every guerilla group uses some form or other of sub-machine gun, but only in small numbers and usually only until enough assault rifles become available for all to use.

The only guerrillas who still employ sub-machine guns on any scale are urban guerrillas. For them the sub-machine gun still has many useful attributes, chief among which is its compact nature and ease of concealment. They tend to use the more modern designs of sub-machine gun, such as the Ingram series or similar compact weapons. The Ingram Model 10 may be taken as typical of many in this group. It is available in 0.45 or 9 mm calibres, and uses what is best described as a 'wrap-around' bolt that reaches forward around the barrel. Thus the overall length can be much reduced compared to more orthodox layouts. Rounds are fed into the weapon from a box magazine inserted upwards through the pistol grip. The resultant layout makes the Model 10 easy to handle and aim, mainly due to the weapon's centre of gravity being over the pistol grip.

The Ingram Model 10 is not the only weapon to use the 'wrap-around' bolt layout. It was first used on the series of Czech sub-machine guns, that started with the vzor 23. Perhaps the most widely-known weapon using the same layout is the Israeli Uzi. All three of these sub-machine guns can be found in urban guerrilla hands, but not in any great numbers. Compared to rural guerrilla numbers, the numbers of urban guerrillas are small and their weapon tallies are correspondingly limited.

If sub-machine gun manufacturers had to rely on guerrillas for their customers, they would probably starve. Yet every year more and more new sub-machine guns appear on the market and seem to find takers. Most go to regular armed forces and their

Left *The Chinese Type 64 silenced sub-machine gun* (T. Gander).

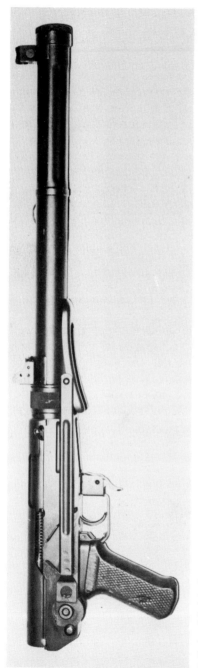

Right *A weapon produced by the North Vietnamese for their guerrilla-based armies, the 7.62 mm Type 50. This sub-machine gun is based on the Soviet PPSh-41 but uses components of many other weapons. Many are still in guerrilla use throughout the Far East.*

special forces off-shoots where the attributes of the sub-machine gun continue to find applications. It is difficult to find reasons to produce silenced sub-machine guns: the only possible users are again the various special forces, and their requirements are limited, but still silenced sub-machine guns are offered for possible sale. Such weapons have obvious attractions for the guerrilla. They cannot be made entirely silent, but they can be made to produce muffled (or 'moderated') firing sounds that can hide a firing location and thus generally confuse an enemy. Once again, the Chinese are the main producers, although other weapons such as the Ingram Model 10 and Czech Skorpion machine pistol can be fitted with extremely effective silencers. By contrast the Chinese 7.62 mm Type 64 was designed from the outset to be a silenced sub-machine gun. In design terms it is something of a dog's dinner, using operating mechanisms and principles taken from many other weapons, all allied to a long silencer that extends some way in front of the barrel muzzle. The silencer seriously affects the ballistics of the bullet so that the effective range is short, at best only just over 100 metres, and combat ranges are much shorter.

The Type 64 has now been joined by the Type 85, a silenced version of the orthodox Type 85 sub-machine gun. Both the Type 64 and Type 85 fire conventional 7.62 x 25 mm pistol ammunition.

There is one variant of the sub-machine gun that requires mention. This is the machine pistol, a hybrid weapon that is really an automatic pistol capable of producing fully automatic burst fire. Since most of these weapons are small and light, the recoil

20

Above *A weapon something between a pistol and a sub-machine gun, the Polish 9 mm PM-63 machine pistol, seen here with its rudimentary butt folded; this weapon has a cyclic rate of fire of 650 rpm (T. Gander).*

Below *The Czech 9 mm M25 with a folding metal stock, a sub-machine gun used throughout the Middle East by various guerrilla groups (T. Gander).*

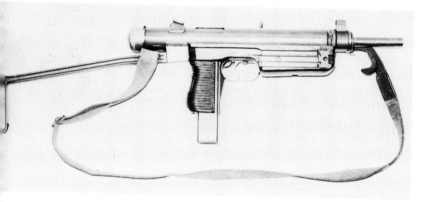

forces produced after firing a few fully automatic shots are enough to force the pistol off its point of aim and waste ammuni-

Below *The Israeli Uzi sub-machine gun, a weapon that is now used around the world, not always in approved hands (T. Gander).*

Above *What can be done: an Ingram M-11 sub-machine gun fitted with a silencer* (T. Gander).

tion. Introducing various forms of butt can gain some form of control over recoil, but such expedients can mitigate against the use of the machine pistol to the point where there are now few examples to quote.

Yet those few examples can be found in guerrilla hands. One is the Soviet 9 mm Stechkin APS. Relatively few of these odd weapons were produced. The few that were made soon passed from Soviet use, and most of them appear to have ended up in the Middle East where some guerrillas or militiamen seem to like the effect their appearance can produce on a crowd. In the Far East numerous fully-automatic versions of the old Mauser C/96 'Broomhandle', now nearly all locally-produced copies, can still be found. There the main attraction again appears to be their appearance and the mark of authority that such weapons can bestow.

MACHINE GUNS

The machine gun is not a universal guerrilla weapon. By nature of its very size, it is a difficult, if not impossible, weapon for the urban guerrilla to employ (other than for special occasions or purposes) yet in rural areas it can be difficult for guerrillas to take on regular or paramilitary forces without the fire support that only machine guns can provide.

It has been mentioned earlier in this book that weapons such as machine guns can be counter-productive in guerrilla warfare. It might make a considerable morale-boosting or attention-grabbing impression to demonstrate that weapons such as heavy machine guns are in the possession of guerrillas, but it is difficult to move or hide heavy machine guns quickly. Attempting to protect them by standing to fight as attempts are made to spirit away heavy machine guns can be a costly operation for guerrillas, so as a general rule the large calibre heavy machine guns are not usually considered for most guerrilla purposes. Heavy machine guns, the types with calibres of 12.7 mm and upwards, and which require large and heavy mountings, are thus used only by relatively large rural guerrilla bands operating in country that can conceal their numbers and their weapons – Afghanistan and Vietnam provide examples of such terrain.

Confined and well-patrolled areas such as Northern Ireland rarely see any form of machine gun in use, by either the IRA or the UDA. Weapons such as American M60s and Browning 0.30 machine guns have been displayed in IRA hands, but mainly for propaganda purposes only. On the few occasions in which they have been used 'operationally' it has usually been from the concealment of closed-bodied commercial vehicles that can move away immediately after opening fire. Even when the machine guns involved have been enhanced with this mobility, they have nearly always been captured within a short time, often with IRA casualties being inflicted in the process.

The IRA experience can be taken as typical, even though machine guns will almost certainly continue to feature in IRA operations from time to time. Only in remote areas where security forces seldom operate or venture can machine guns be used to any real effect by guerrillas carrying out the normal run of guerrilla operations. But should any guerrilla force decide to stand up and fight it out in normal combat with security forces, machine guns will be essential – machine guns will almost certainly be used against them.

Guerrilla machine guns fall into two main categories, the light machine gun (LMG) and the general purpose machine gun (GPMG). The LMG, despite its name, is not a lightweight weapon, as the general weight is around 9 kg and it is inclined to be bulky. It uses an air-cooled barrel. Most models employ some form of magazine for the ammunition feed. By contrast, the GPMG is a dual-purpose weapon, intended to be used as a LMG when fitted with a bipod. or as a heavy machine gun (HMG) to produce sustained fire (SF, hence GPMG(SF)) when mounted on a sturdy tripod. Again, all examples in use today have air-cooled barrels, but use belt-fed ammunition rather than a magazine; some models are able to use both.

Guerrillas rarely use GPMGs in their tripod-mounted form. Instead they use them as LMGs most of the time. The only time GPMGs seem to get placed upon any form of heavy mounting is when they are used against low-flying aircraft or helicopters. Generally speaking, GPMGs employed as LMGs are slightly heavier and bulkier than purpose-built LMGs. These days purpose-built LMGs are coming back into fashion, after a period when the GPMG prevailed.

Again, dealing in general terms, the LMG is a squad support weapon. The GPMG in the tripod-mounted GPMG(SF) role is usually employed as a general fire support weapon at company level or above. Thus the GPMG(SF) has little tactical utility for the guerrilla, operating as they usually do in small and highly mobile groups.

As with all other weapon types, guerrillas have to use what they can obtain. For many groups their machine-guns come via Soviet supply routes and thus consist of Soviet-designed weapons, even though the place of production or supply origin varies widely.

A form of LMG known to be widely used by guerrillas is the Soviet RPK. At first sight the RPK looks like an AK-47, which is not surprising for that is exactly what it is. The RPK is an enlarged AK-47 fitted with a longer and heavier barrel, a bipod and an increased capacity magazine. It is used as a squad fire support weapon and is thus fitted with a 40-round curved box magazine or a 75-round drum; it can also accommodate

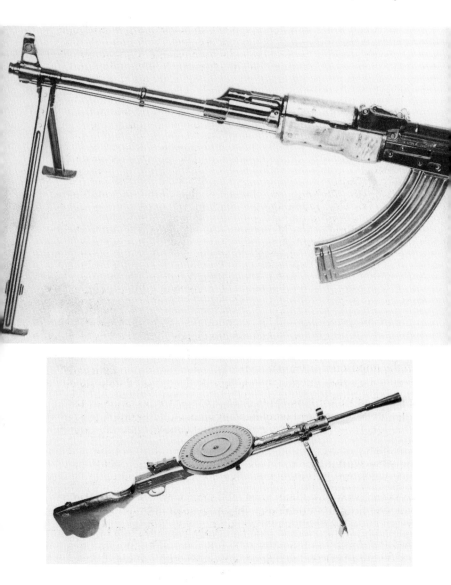

standard AK-47 or AKM 30-round magazines.

The RPK is light, weighing only 5 kg by itself, and it does have
limitations. One is the barrel, which cannot be changed when
prolonged burst firing makes it too hot to fire safely. Bursts of fire
therefore have to be short, and strict user-imposed fire discipline

Left *The Soviet 7.62 mm RPK light machine gun, a weapon obviously developed from the AK-47 assault rifle* (T. Gander).

Below left *Another veteran still likely to be used by guerrillas, the Soviet 7.62 mm Degtyarev DP light machine gun with its distinctive 47-round flat drum magazine* (T. Gander).

has to be imposed to ensure that the barrel temperature limits are not exceeded; combat experience has demonstrated that guerrillas often ignore this restriction and wreck the weapon in the process. In practice, the barrel heating limitation means that the RPK's cyclic rate of fire of 660 rpm is reduced to a practical 80 rpm or less.

Yugoslav light machine guns closely allied to the RPK are known as the Model M72B1 and M72AB1.

Other Soviet LMGs likely to be encountered in guerrilla hands are the old Second World War DPM and the RPD. The DPM can trace its origins back to 1926, and is easily recognised by the flat circular magazine over the receiver. The DPM fires the old 7.62 x 54 mm rimmed cartridge. (The Chinese version of the RPD is known as the Type 53.)

By contrast, the RPD fires the intermediate-powered 7.62 x 39 mm cartridge, and is one of the most commonly encountered Soviet LMGs in guerrilla hands. The RPD is a LMG weighing only 7.1 kg unloaded and is fed from a 100-round link belt, normally carried in a drum magazine located under the gun. This

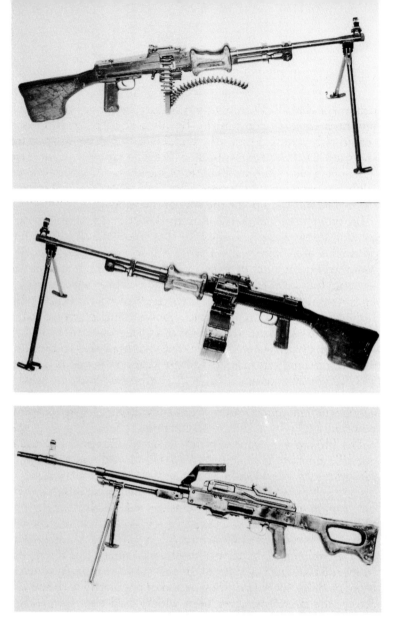

Top *Seen here with a belt feed, the Soviet 7.62 mm RPD light machine gun (T. Gander).*

Middle *An RPD with its 100-round ammunition belt carried in a drum magazine (T. Gander).*

Bottom *Despite its appearance the Soviet 7.62 mm PK machine gun is a true general purpose machine gun and is shown here in its light machine gun form (T. Gander).*

drum is a good RPD recognition feature; another is the bipod mounted close to the muzzle. By all accounts the RPD is a remarkably robust design, which makes it a valuable weapon for the guerrillas operating in parts of Africa and South-East Asia where guerrilla RPDs proliferate. Some of the South-East Asia RPDs are probably ex-Chinese. The Chinese RPD is still offered for sale as the Type 56 or the similar Type 56-1.

Perhaps the best of all the current Soviet machine-guns is the weapon known simply as the PK. This is really a GPMG (it has a rapid-change air-cooled barrel) capable of being used or mounted in a number of ways, including as an armoured vehicle weapon, but for a GPMG it is remarkably light, weighing only 9 kg in its empty and basic form; the later PKM has a weight of only 8.4 kg. The PK is a remarkable weapon in many ways, one being that the gas-operated mechanism and feed system use only a few moving parts. There are thus fewer components to break or wear out. Ammunition is fed into the weapon from belts holding 100, 200 or 250 rounds. The belts can be fed directly into the weapon, although a belt box slung under the receiver is a useful accessory. The ammunition fired continues to be the old full-powered 7.62 x 54 mm rimmed cartridge.

The PK has a cyclic rate of fire of up to 720 rpm. The usual guerrilla version is mounted on a bipod and can be readily recognized by its skeleton butt stock. Most guerrillas seem to dispense with the belt box and carry their ammunition belts hanging loose. More ammunition is carried in belts slung about the person. A Chinese copy of the PK is known as the Type 80.

By contrast models of Western machine guns used by guerrillas are relatively few. The closest Western equivalent of the squad support RPK light machine gun is the old Browning Automatic Rifle, or BAR. Despite its long period of popularity with the US Army, the BAR has never been widely used elsewhere (other than in Belgium and Poland prior to 1940), for it is an odd hybrid weapon. It has been referred to as a machine rifle, as its burst fire capability is limited by the 20-round capacity of the box magazine employed. It is also heavy, weighing 8.7 kg, and lacks a quick-change barrel. BARs may still be encountered in guerrilla use, but the numbers involved must be few. Those few are probably only retained until something better turns up.

Old American machine guns that keep cropping up in guerrilla use include variants of the 0.30 Model 1919. This weapon, with its distinctive perforated air-cooled barrel jacket, was produced in the millions during the Second World War for applications that varied from aircraft to armoured vehicle installations. Ground mountings were supposed to use tripods, but infantry squad fire support requirements dictated the use of a bipod. The result was the M1919A6, an awkward weapon with a rudimentary butt and bipod. This improvisation became accepted as standard, but even before it was produced during the Second World War, numerous irregular forces had started making their own modifications to aircraft and armoured vehicle machine guns to make them suitable for their own purposes. Some of these improvisations still survive, but they are not popular weapons. The M1919 is too heavy and awkward a load to be carried or fired using anything other than heavy mountings. Still, the M1919 has been flourished in front of the Press in Northern Ireland, and has been used by guerrillas in Central and South America, South East Asia and parts of Africa.

The more modern M60, another American weapon is also used by guerrillas. The M60 is a belt-fed GPMG that has not proved to be too great a success, for it is a poor GPMG(SF) weapon, and far too heavy and awkward to be a viable LMG; weight as a LMG is over 10.5 kg. However it was used by the US armed forces throughout the Vietnam War, and from there inevitably fell into guerrilla hands. From South East Asia, guerrilla M60s have spread to nearly all parts of the world. The supply line was swollen by a series of thefts from American National Guard arsenals, probably with the IRA as the intended end user. Numbers of M60s did turn up in Northern Ireland several years ago but most were captured or found by the security forces before they could do too much damage. Some of those captured M60s were found to originate from National Guard stocks. Since that time, more M60s are known to have arrived in Northern Ireland, but the numbers involved have been small.

European machine gun types in use by guerrillas are many. They vary from pre-1945 German MG 42s to modern Czech weapons. The MG 42s originally came from old Second World War booty, or from stocks originally taken over by victorious Resistance groups. Before 1945 the MG 42, a GPMG, was acknowledged to be one of the finest of all machine gun designs, · and it is still good enough to remain in current production as the West German Rheinmetall MG3, now chambered for 7.62 x 51

Above A .30 Browning M1919A4 machine gun, an air-cooled weapon now generally passing from favour but still used by many guerrilla organizations.

Right A Browning M1919A4 on its tripod (T. Gander).

Below Another odd hybrid weapon, the Browning Automatic Rifle, here an M1918A2. The 20-round magazine limits burst fire and the weapon is heavy but it is still widely used by many military forces, both official and unofficial (T. Gander).

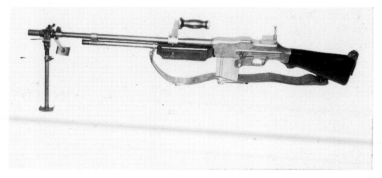

Guerrilla Warfare Weapons

Below *A pre-1945 German 7.92 mm MG42, seen here with its feed plate open.*

Below right *Despite its age the Czech 7.92 mm ZB-26 light machine gun is still widely used, with users including guerrilla organizations.*

mm NATO ammunition. The original MG 42 fired the German 7.92 x 57 mm cartridge. This cartridge is still used by the Yugoslav Model M53 GPMG, a direct copy of the original MG 42, right down to the types of mountings available.

After 1945 MG 42s were used by many regular armed forces and once they were replaced by weapons chambered for the new NATO rounds, the MG 42s joined the international arms trade circuit. From there they ended up in some very odd places. They are still being captured by security forces in Southern Africa (the South African defence forces have captured many MG 42s from SWAPO), further north in the Sub-Saharan region, and in the Horn of Africa. Despite its age, the MG 42 looks like remaining in guerrilla use for some time to come. It is still an excellent weapon that continues to keep on working, even though its construction relies mainly on sheet metal stampings and welds.

Another European veteran is the Czech ZB 26. The design dates from the mid-1920s and was the predecessor of the British Bren Gun. The ZB 26 is a LMG originally chambered for the 7.92 x 57 mm cartridge, and was produced for the Germans as well as the Czechs until 1945. After 1945 captured stocks followed the usual path into guerrilla hands, but many more came from the Far East. There the ZB 26 had for long been a favourite weapon of the then ruling Chinese Kuomintang forces. Once the Kuomintang had been overthrown, in 1949, huge numbers of ZB

Right *Top, a Czech 7.92 mm ZB-26 light machine gun with a Bren Gun, a weapon developed from the ZB-26, underneath.*

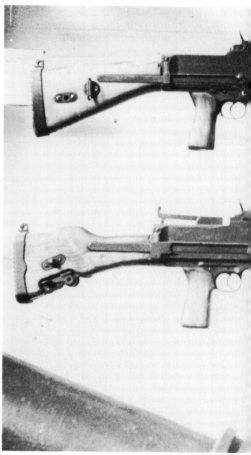

Below *The Vz52 light machine gun is a post-war Czech development of the earlier ZB-26 light machine gun and can be encountered in a number of models firing a variety of different cartridges (T. Gander).*

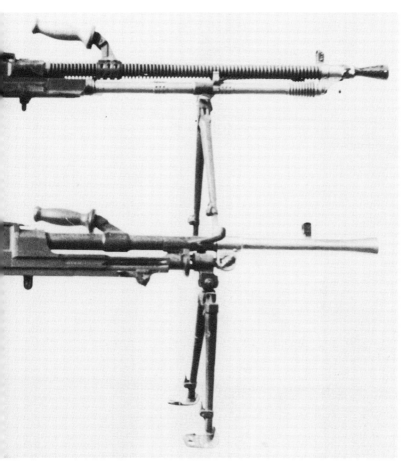

26 LMGs were dumped on the open market. They are still excellent and sturdy weapons that are now limited in their utility only by their ammunition supply.

Since 1945 the Czechs have continued to produce machine guns to their own designs. Their 7.62 mm vzor 59 still bears some resemblance to the pre-war ZB 26, but it is now a belt-fed GPMG. Some of these weapons have been encountered in guerrilla use in the Middle East.

Although produced in far greater numbers than the original Czech ZB 26, the British Bren Gun is little used by guerrillas. The main reason for this is that it is still in service with many regular armed forces throughout the world. Any old war-period

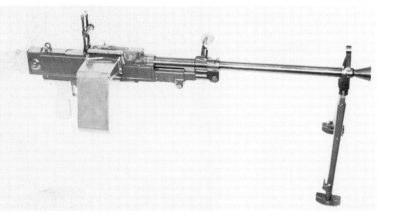

The Czech Vz59N is a general purpose machine gun that has found customers throughout the Middle East (T. Gander).

0.303 Brens that come on to the market are snapped up by arms dealers for conversion to the 7.62 mm NATO calibre and resale to regular armed forces, who continue to value the Bren's reliability and excellent handling attributes – arms dealers with guerrilla end users in mind can hardly get a look in. Thus the only Brens in irregular use are the odd few that remain on the guerrilla arms supply circuit, originating from old Empire campaigns such as Malaya and Cyprus.

Although they are used by only the most organized and established guerrilla groups, some mention must be made of heavy machine-guns. As already outlined, these have calibres of 12.7 mm and upwards but only two weapons will be mentioned here. One is the 0.50 Browning M2, an air-cooled weapon making a definite comeback after years of relative neglect. The neglect has nearly all been engendered by the M2s great weight (the gun alone weighs over 39 kg) and bulk, but the realization has again been made that the projectile fired by the M2 is a prodigious man-stopper. Modern technology has produced a new range of ammunition types that can perforate useful depths of armour and can carry explosive or incendiary warheads. Thus the M2, originally produced during the 1920s, is once more in mass production, and the ammunition is a NATO standard (12.7 x 99 mm).

All this is usually lost on the guerrilla. For him the M2 is

Right *A true heavy machine gun, the Soviet 12.7 mm DShK machine gun on its anti-aircraft tripod mounting.*

Below *A 12.7 mm DShK heavy machine gun on its wheeled ground mounting.*

usually too much of a handful. But if he is harried by aircraft or helicopters the M2 takes on a new importance, for even within NATO the M2 is regarded as a viable anti-aircraft weapon. The mountings involved may be large and heavy, but they are effective, so M2s are once again in use by guerrilla groups as disparate as Lebanese militias and Burmese Karens.

The Soviet equivalent to the M2 is the 12.7 mm DShK-38.

The usual mounting for this weapon is a heavy wheeled carriage that sometimes features a shield. The carriage can be configured to become an anti-aircraft mounting, for the DShK-38 is another weapon effective against low-flying aircraft and helicopters. The two-wheeled carriage helps considerably when moving the DShK-38 around over flat ground. This makes it more mobile than similar weapons, such as the Browning M2, that usually lack wheels.

Both the DShK-38 and M2 are effective weapons at ranges up to 2,000 metres. Both can be used against targets such as soft-skinned vehicles, light structures and even some light armoured vehicles. For guerrillas, they are also particularly useful against targets such as aircraft and helicopters on the ground. When fired against such targets heavy machine guns can be very effective weapons, but they are also relatively immobile and thus of limited value for many guerrilla groups, who have to keep moving to survive.

MORTARS

The mortar is an indirect fire weapon that was resurrected during the First World War to become an infantry weapon for use in the trenches. Once re-established, the tactical use altered from being a form of front-line light artillery to becoming a portable infantry support weapon. The mortar is widely used today, for its tactical attributes are many. It is relatively light and portable, it can deliver useful explosive or other payloads at a high angle, and it is fairly simple to use. When used against protected or unsuspecting targets the surprise effect of mortar bombs can be more damaging to security force morale than the physical harm actually inflicted.

For guerrillas, the mortar has several attractions. One is its combination of portability and firepower. Guerrillas can rarely own or use any form of artillery, but the mortar comes pretty close to artillery, especially when used in hilly country. The time required to get a mortar in and out of action can be quite short, usually much less than for a comparable artillery weapon. An 81 or 82 mm mortar bomb can carry an explosive payload of anything from 0.4 to 0.9 kg of explosive which, when combined with the fragmentation effect of the bomb itself, can have a considerable impact on any target. Mortars can also fire incendiary, smoke and other types of ammunition. Rates of fire can be quite high; for medium mortars, over 20 bombs a minute is not uncommon.

Limitations imposed by the mortar on guerrilla users are much the same as those for heavy machine-guns. Mortars are bulky and heavy weapons (other than the really light mortars), and are difficult to transport or hide without notice. They also require some skill and training to use properly, but even under ideal conditions they are really area rather than point target weapons. Their high ballistic trajectory and the number of variables inherent in firing mortars accurately means they can only be used against large targets such as villages or supply installations.

Guerrilla mortars fall into four main categories: light, medium, heavy and home-made. Dealing with the light mortars first, these usually have calibres of 51 mm or 60 mm, with the accent on the latter. These light mortars may use simple bipods and baseplates, or they may be of the 'Commando' type which lack any form of bipod or other barrel support, and have only small or rudimentary baseplates. The latter are much favoured by guerrillas, because they are one-man loads and require no more setting up than placing the baseplate on the ground, loading a bomb and aiming and holding the barrel by hand. The bomb is usually launched using a trigger mechanism. There are numerous examples of this simple approach. Perhaps the most prolific manufacturers are the French concern of Thomson-Brandt, who produce a range of 60 mm Commando mortars. Others are produced in Finland, Belgium, Chile, Spain, Israel, Yugoslavia and South Africa.

The other form of light mortar is exemplified by the Chinese 60 mm Type 63. This small and widely-used weapon has an interesting history for it was originally based on a French mortar produced in 1935. The Americans copied the French original direct, and used it throughout the Second World War as the M2.

Right *An old idea that might reappear one day . . . what appears to be a small entrenching tool is in fact a mortar that doubles as a spade. On this illustration a is the 37 mm barrel, c is a muzzle cap attached to a monopod leg, d is a barrel support sleeve against which the support monopod rests, f is a gas bleed collar used to vary the range, while g is the base plate.*

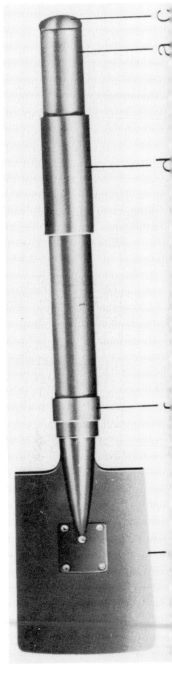

Below *The top end of the guerrilla market, a 120 mm Model 38 heavy mortar.*

Left *A typical light mortar, the Soviet 50 mm Model M40 (T. Gander).*

After 1945 the M2 was copied by the Chinese Nationalists. In their turn the Chinese Communists took over the design, adding their own modifications. These involved keeping the baseplate and bipod permanently attached to the barrel on hinges, and adding a carrying handle. Sometimes the bipod is removed completely. The Type 63 can thus be carried into action by one man, who has only to unfold the bipod and baseplate by a flick of the wrist and the weapon is ready to emplace and load. During the Vietnam War the Type 63 was frequently used to attack base areas and airfields. It could be carried into action, six or seven bombs could be launched, and the guerrillas could be up and off before the first bomb had landed. Complete, a Type 63 weighs 12.4 kg and fires an HE bomb weighing around 1.5 kg. There is also a lighter Type 63-1 weighing only 11.5 kg.

The main drawback to the light mortars is their relatively short range. This is usually limited to 1,800 metres at best, and to only 1,000 metres or so for the Commando models. At such ranges accuracy can be poor. The bombs involved are small and light, and have limited payloads.

Medium mortars have calibres of 81 or 82 mm, the latter being the Warsaw Pact standard, the former the same for NATO. These mortars are usually the upper limit for most guerrilla groups, for weight starts to intrude. The weight comes from the heavy steel barrel, the bipod and sighting unit and the large baseplate, which might be circular or rectangular. The Soviet 82 mm 82-PM 37, very widely used by guerrillas, weighs 56 kg emplaced for action. Even if the mortar is broken down into its three main components, each component can be a hefty load, to say nothing of the ammunition. Some guerrillas use mules or other pack animals to carry their mortars, others rely on manpower. In parts of Africa some guerrillas solve the portability problem by carrying the component loads on their heads. The Soviet 82-PM 37, which may be taken as typical for this category, has a range of 3,000 metres and fires bombs weighing just over 3 kg. Up to 25 bombs a minute can be fired, but only for short periods.

The weight problem with medium mortars can be reduced by leaving off items such as the sight unit or the bipod. Some guerrillas make a practice of resting the barrel on its baseplate by hand, leaving aiming and stability to simply holding the barrel manually. Needless to say, such measures do little to enhance

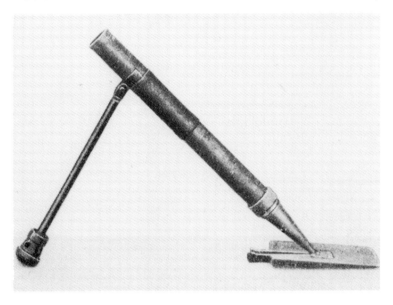

The Second World War Soviet 37 mm spade mortar fully assembled. This weapon was carried by the Soviet Partisans but it was not used on a large scale.

accuracy, but they can be effective enough when firing at area targets. What happens when the barrel gets hot from prolonged firing is another matter.

Heavy mortars have only one calibre, namely 120 mm. They are large bulky weapons that are rarely used by guerrillas, other than in locations such as Afghanistan where numbers of captured Soviet 120-HM 43 mortars have been used by the Mujahadeen. These weapons weigh over 280 kg when emplaced, which means moving them is a major task. They can be towed on two-wheeled carriages, which brings their weight up to 500 kg or more. Range is up to 5,700 metres or so, and the bombs weigh over 15 kg.

With home-made mortars, one is moving very much into guerrilla territory. Guerrillas produce mortars only when they either lack access to purpose-built weapons, or when they have a particular application that cannot be met by another means. To actually produce a mortar is simple. All that is required is a steel tube and something to absorb the recoil forces produced on firing. Home made mortars produced by those masters of guerrilla tactics, the British Home Guard of 1940-'44, were usually steel pipes set into timber baulks at a fixed angle.

The problem when producing home made mortars is the ammunition. Mortar bombs are more complex than they first appear. Attempts to produce such items using the facilities available to most guerrillas often means nothing more than a tin packed with home-produced explosive, and a crude pressure or burning fuze. These 'bombs' are launched using black powder, with aiming and fuze timing usually left to luck.

The latest examples of home-made mortars come from Northern Ireland, although many other guerrilla organizations have attempted to produce similar weapons. Northern Ireland mortars are usually large calibre devices using steel tubes arranged on timber racks carried on the backs of hijacked vehicles. The main targets are security forces barracks or installations protected by high barriers and wire mesh erected as protection against direct fire weapons.

The bombs are usually crude metal canisters or finned pipes packed with explosive and fitted with basic pressure or timing devices. The vehicle is driven into position near the intended target, with the pre-loaded mortar tubes hidden under a tarpaulin. On the firing site the covers are removed and the mortars set off by slow-burning fuzes or some form of timer.

The mortars have to be deployed in multiples (nine or ten is usual), because accuracy is poor and many bombs have to be fired for there to be any chance of a hit. Another factor dictating multiples is that many of the bombs are inevitably 'duds' that will not explode as arranged.

If they should explode on target, the effects of the home-made bombs can be devastating, but thankfully many IRA mortar bomb attacks have turned out to be complete failures, and some have been counter-productive by hitting 'civilian' targets. Overall it could be said that the effort and facilities devoted by the IRA to manufacturing and deploying their home-made mortars could have been put to more productive use. For other guerrilla forces, there is no recourse but to produce their own mortars to attack their targets, so home-produced mortars will continue to be guerrilla weapons for the forseeable future.

MISSILES AND HEAVY WEAPONS

When mention is made of missiles and heavy weapons in guerrilla terms, it should be appreciated that such weapons are not a normal part of the usual guerrilla armoury. Nearly all guerrilla campaigns carried out until recently were conducted without the help of anything other than hand-held weapons and, at most, machine guns and mortars. Missiles, guided or unguided, were uncommon and have only recently been introduced to the guerrilla armoury. Heavy weapons impose many limitations on mobility and concealment, and until recently were thus largely ignored.

Modern technology has now caught up with the guerrilla. In some parts of the world no self-respecting guerrilla movement seems to have any local credibility unless it is tooled up with the latest shiny weapons hot from the production lines. Some of these modern weapons are well-suited to the guerrilla's environment. Others are not.

We will deal with missiles first.

Unguided missiles

Military missiles come in two forms, guided and unguided. Unguided missiles have been around for longer, and are generally classified as rockets projected from some form of launcher device. The classic example is the artillery rocket, which is still widely employed by guerrillas all around the world.

The artillery rocket is an ancient weapon that came back into prominence during the Second World War. It was then used, as it still is, as an auxiliary to conventional artillery, and was used to beef up bombardments by being launched in salvos intended to saturate large areas with explosives. The classic Second World War launcher was the Soviet Katyuscha, a multiple rail system carried on a truck. While many guerrillas would dearly like to possess the firepower potential of such a weapons system, the Katyuscha is too large and obvious a device for normal guerrilla operation. But the rockets fired by the Katyuscha-type launchers are another matter.

Pre-1945 artillery rockets had calibres of around 82 mm or so, and ranges were limited. Improved technology produced longer ranges and larger calibre rockets, to the point where two calibres are now in use by various guerrilla groups, 140 mm and 122 mm.

The 140 mm rockets are Soviet in origin, and are normally launched in multiples from tubes carried on a truck. Guerrillas fire the 140 mm rockets from single tubes mounted on a flat board. The board is placed on the ground, the tube muzzle is elevated by building up a heap of soil or gravel until the correct launch angle is obtained, and the rocket is then fired electrically from a distance. Each rocket weights 39.6 kg and carries an 18.8 kg explosive warhead. Maximum range is 9,800 metres.

Soviet-designed 122 mm rockets can also use individual launcher tubes, but with this rocket a more formal launcher tripod can be provided. This makes the rocket much easier to aim for any hope of accuracy. Range is over 10,000 metres and each rocket weighs 45.8 kg. Of this, 19.4 kg is explosive.

Other types of artillery rocket are in use by guerrillas, but the above-mentioned pair are by far the most commonly encountered. Despite their weight they can be man-carried to a launch site for firing against distant targets, but it should be appreciated that such rockets fired individually have little chance of hitting a specific target, other than at very short ranges. The

rocket is an inherently inaccurate weapon, so any rockets launched individually can have little more than nuisance or propaganda value.

But as nuisance weapons they are ideal for many guerrillas. They were used extensively by guerrilla groups in South-East Asia from 1945 onwards, and at one time they were used extensively by Palestine Liberation Organization (PLO) guerrillas operating against Israeli settlements close to the borders of Lebanon and Syria. For years the Israeli settlers had to live under a drizzle of PLO rockets launched at irregular intervals, often at night. Few rockets actually hit anything, but they constituted a constant danger to life and property that meant a whole generation of Israeli 'border' children had to be educated and brought up largely from within underground shelters.

Not all guerrilla rockets are launched individually. A few of the larger and better organized guerrilla groups have access to multiple rocket launchers. Typical of these groups are the ever-active Afghan Mujahadeen, who have somehow obtained numbers of Chinese 107 mm Type 63 12-tube artillery rocket launchers and the rockets to go with them. The PLO have also used this weapon system in the Middle East.

The Type 63 launcher can be fired from the back of a light truck, but is more often deployed by guerrillas on a light two-

The Chinese 107 mm Type 63 12-round rocket launcher has been used by the Mujahadeen and has a maximum range of 8,500 metres.

wheeled carriage that is sometimes fitted with bicycle wheels, to reduce weight as much as possible. For firing, the wheels can be removed to rest the launcher on a firing platform under the carriage. When loaded and ready to fire the Type 63 weighs just over 600 kg. Each rocket weighs 18.8 kg and has a maximum range of 8,500 metres (incendiary rockets have a slightly shorter range). The Type 63 and its rockets have often been used to good effect inside Afghanistan, but unless careful prior preparations for a hasty withdrawal have been made, weapons such as the Type 63 tend to be one-shot weapons. In both the Middle East

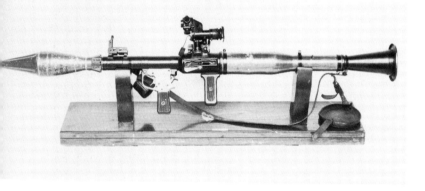

Above *A Soviet-produced RPG-7 anti-tank rocket launcher complete with its optical sight (T. Gander).*

Below *The lower rocket launcher shown here is the Soviet RPG-2, complete with its rocket; the upper launcher is a Chinese Type 56, a copy of the RPG-2. The launcher tube has a calibre of 80 mm and fires a rocket weighing around 1.85 kg. (T. Gander).*

Below right *The American M72 rocket launcher uses a disposable launcher tube that is telescoped open for firing, as shown here.*

and Afghanistan a rapid response from the security forces under fire has often meant that the launchers have had to be abandoned after firing just one salvo.

PLO guerrillas operating from within Lebanon prior to the 1982 Israeli invasion of that country produced their own improvised mobile six- or nine-tube 122 mm launchers, mounted on light commercial trucks. Some of the rockets and launchers involved came from North Korea or Egypt.

Artillery rockets are long-range weapons. Guerrillas also use a number of types of rocket as short-range anti-armour weapons. One of the most widely-used of these anti-armour weapons is known as the RPG-7. This is a Soviet-designed 40 mm calibre launcher that fires a rocket with an oversize hollow charge warhead. It was developed from an earlier weapon known as the RPG-2, many of which remain in guerrilla service wherever Soviet influence has spread. The rocket weighs 2.25 kg and uses an 85 mm diameter warhead that is effective against lightly-armoured vehicles and structures such as blockhouses. The weight of a complete RPG-7 loaded is 10.15 kg.

The RPG-7 is fired from the shoulder. Most launchers have a one-piece launcher tube, but more recent versions have a two-piece tube to reduce the carrying bulk. The firer is provided with what at first glance appears to be a complicated optical sight incorporating a range-finder and for in-flight stability the rocket is provided with tail fins that fold out after launch. The maximum range against static targets is 500 metres. Cross winds can affect accuracy, and the rocket can be detonated before it reaches its target by erecting stand-off metal mesh barriers around a potential target area. Thus many internal security vehicles (and buildings) can be seen covered by wire mesh screens, to protect them from the worst effects of RPG-7 rockets.

Although the RPG-7 is Soviet in origin it has been produced

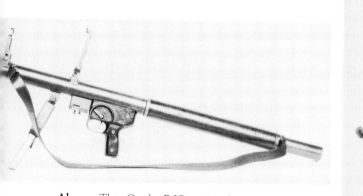

Above *The Czech P-27 anti-tank grenade launcher is also known as the 'Pancerovka' and fires a rocket weighing 3.75 kg that can penetrate up to 250 mm of armour* (T. Gander).

elsewhere. The Chinese Type 69 is a direct copy and Pakistan also produces a RPG-7 clone. The Czech P-27 is based on the earlier RPG-2, a Soviet design which is a much simpler weapon than the RPG-7, with a range limited to 150 metres at the most. The Chinese version of the RPG-2 is known as the Type 56.

The closest equivalent to the RPG-7 used in the West is the American 66 mm M72. This one-shot weapon differs in many respects from the RPG-7, for it is a telescopic tube firing a 66 mm calibre rocket. The tube is telescoped open for firing and when opened, simple flip-up sights unfold. If the launcher is not fired for any reason it can be telescoped shut again for use another time.

The M72 is now regarded by most NATO armed forces as obsolete, for its 66 mm warhead is no longer effective against the armour of most modern battle tanks. However, it remains effective against light armoured vehicles and structures and is thus a viable guerrilla weapon. Many guerrilla forces have obtained M72s and as more are withdrawn from front-line military use they will inevitably pass increasingly into guerrilla service. They are handy weapons. They weigh only 2.36 kg and have a range against static targets of 300 metres.

The M72 has been copied: even the Soviet Union has used the basic design of the M72 to produce their RPG-18. The Yugoslavs produce a near copy with a calibre of 64 mm, known as the RBR-M80. The RPG-75 is a Czech 68 mm weapon apparently based on the Soviet RPG-18.

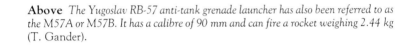

Above *The Yugoslav RB-57 anti-tank grenade launcher has also been referred to as the M57A or M57B. It has a calibre of 90 mm and can fire a rocket weighing 2.44 kg* (T. Gander).

There are many other anti-armour missile weapons in guerrilla armouries. Most are based on the American Bazooka concept, exemplified by the 3.5-inch (88.9 mm) M20. This rocket launcher has for long been out of front-line service with most armed forces, but it is still an effective weapon. It is a long two-section aluminium tube joined together to form a shoulder launcher. A rocket is loaded into the rear and fired electrically by a hand-operated magneto. The maximum anti-armour range for firing the 4 kg rocket is 110 metres. A Chinese-produced copy, still in use in the Far East, is known as the Type 51.

While all these unguided missile systems based on the rocket can be extremely effective guerrilla weapons, they all have one tactical drawback. As the rocket is fired, the exhaust gases kick up clouds of dust and debris that indicate to an enemy exactly where the firing position is located. The same exhaust gases also prevent rockets from being fired from within closed areas, such as building interiors or from inside vehicles, that is unless the firer wants to become a casualty. The same fate will befall anyone caught in the area directly to the rear of a launcher as it is fired. The size of the rear danger area will vary with the type and calibre of the rocket involved, but is seldom less than 30 metres. These restrictions can limit the use of rockets in many tactical situations.

Guided missiles

There are only a few guided missiles in guerrilla use, all air
defence weapons. Two systems predominate, the American
Stinger and the Soviet SA-7. The Soviet SA-7 is the most
numerous.

Many guerrillas would like to use anti-aircraft guided weapons
to remove the threat to their operations imposed by the use of
aircraft and helicopters. Aircraft can observe their movements,
attack their villages, supply lines and bases, and generally harass
and disrupt. The only weapon the guerrilla usually has for
defence against such attacks is the machine gun, which has
serious limitations regarding effective range and lethality against
airborne targets.

The main drawback for any guerrilla organization thinking of
using guided missiles is the cost. Even a relatively simple and un-
sophisticated shoulder-launched missile system can cost tens of
thousands of dollars, so unless a guerrilla organisation has very
rich sponsors or an unlimited supply of money, ground-to-air
missiles are unlikely to be available.

Once obtained, guided missiles require training and sensible
employment. The operator of a SA-7 has to go through a complex firing sequence before the missile is fired. If the sequence is
botched, the firing will be useless. The only way such a sequence
can be learned and carried out reliably is by careful training and
self discipline, both factors that are often lacking in some of the
less-sophisticated guerrilla groups. The British Blowpipe is
another air defence missile system that requires careful training.
After launch, the missile is guided towards its target by actuating
a small thumb-operated joystick. Controlling the joystick is not
an easily-acquired skill. Considerable practice is required, yet
most guerrillas are unlikely to be able to obtain such skills. Even
so, Blowpipes have turned up in Afghanistan, although from
what national source is still uncertain.

There is also the question of correct employment. It has been
observed that many partly- or ill-disciplined guerrilla groups will
go out of their way to fire off whatever weapons they have, at any
opportunity that arises. This is generally known as the 'Beirut
syndrome'. The extreme example of this is available on any
newsreel from Beirut, where so-called militiamen can be observed firing off all the ammunition at their disposal at whatever
seems like a target. While dangerous and wasteful of ammuni-

tion, this practice matters little in combat terms, but when guided missiles are involved such activities take on a more serious aspect.

Simply firing off an air defence missile at the first aircraft target that presents itself usually means that a precious asset is simply wasted, because the operator wants to see what happens or because it seemed a good idea at the time. In areas such as Angola and Afghanistan numerous missiles have been wasted against aerial targets that were either well out of range or were simply flying by and not presenting a threat to anyone. Once a air defence missile has been fired, there is all too often nothing to replace it, so actually selecting and timing the best instant at which to use a missile takes considerable skill and judgement.

Guerrilla possession of an air defence missile is therefore not always an indication that there is a threat to aircraft. Yet guerrillas have been able to employ air defence missiles to considerable effect. In Afghanistan the introduction of American Stinger missiles to Mujahadeen hands (they have also used SA-7s) has meant that there are areas over which Soviet helicopters have operated in constant dread of missile attack. At times, Soviet air activity was severely restricted, and over one period during 1987 one Soviet helicopter was reportedly shot down every day. In Angola, Unita guerrillas have used Stingers successfully, to the extent that the Angolan air force has been unwilling to fly over Unita-controlled areas. In Central America, Nicaraguan helicopters have been brought down by Contra missiles.

There is one further aspect of guerrilla employment of ground-to-air guided missiles, and that involves guerrilla factions operating as terrorists. There have already been several attempts by guerrilla groups to shoot down civilian airliners as they make their landing approaches to civilian airports. Most of the reported attempts have involved one or other of the many PLO factions using SA-7s to bring down El-Al aircraft. Thankfully, all attempts to date have been thwarted by security measures, but it may only be a matter of time before another attempt involving surface-to-air missiles is successful.

The Soviet SA-7 missile system, also known by its NATO name of Grail, has been widely issued to, or somehow obtained by, several guerrilla groups in Africa and the Middle East. Others have cropped up in South East Asia, at least some coming from Chinese sources where the SA-7 is produced as the HN--5A. Egypt also produces a close copy of the SA-7, known as the Sakr Eye. Many armed forces employ the SA-7. The list includes North Korea, Peru, Iraq, Cuba, Cyprus, Iran, Syria and Uganda, to name but a few.

The design of the SA-7 is now well over 20 years old and employs the infra-red signature of an aircraft target to guide its 9 kg missile towards a target. So that the missile will find a target to home on to, the operator has to ensure that the missile is 'locked on' a target before it is fired. This involves a definite pre-launch sequence that commences by switching on a thermal battery to power the system. The battery takes a little time to warm up and power the missile electronics and the infra-red seeker head on the missile. The seeker head also takes a short time to operate. The operator is then told that the missile is ready to fire by an indicator light in the simple optical sight. Once the missile is launched, it tail-chases the target and destroys it with the 2.5 kg explosive and fragmentation warhead.

This operating sequence, although simple, involves self-discipline and training if the missile is not to be wasted. Even when launched, the SA-7 infra-red seeker head can be thwarted by the release of flares from the target aircraft, and other ploys, but the SA-7 has proved to be remarkably effective against low-flying aircraft. Helicopters make even better targets for the SA-7.

The American counterpart to the SA-7 is now the Stinger. Stingers in use by the Contras, the Mujahadeen and Unita have all come direct from the United States under one disguise or another, and they have proved to be more effective than the SA-7. They are certainly easier to operate and use and, weighing only 13.4 kg, are lighter to carry than the SA-7 (weight nearly 20 kg). The long, slender missile is supersonic in flight and employs the passive infra-red guidance principle, but the range of the missile has never been officially disclosed – it is thought to be about 4,000 metres. It is known that the Stinger missile can attack a target from any angle, rather than the somewhat restricted tail-chase attack of the SA-7.

The British Blowpipe has already been mentioned. Exactly how these missiles came to be in the hands of the Afghan Mujahadeen has yet to be discovered, but the numbers involved appear to have been few and were probably the result of a one-off hand-out from a sympathetic Islamic government. From the few reports that have filtered through regarding Blowpipe's combat performance in Afghanistan, they do not appear to have been very popular weapons. For a start, Blowpipe is bulkier and heavier (20.7 kg) than either Stinger or the SA-7. As it is guided in flight by the operator using a thumb-actuated joystick, Blowpipe is much more difficult to control. In trained hands, such as during the 1982 Falklands campaign, Blowpipe has proved to be a very effective air defence weapon. In untrained hands it has proved to be less so.

Anti-aircraft guns

In terms of sheer bulk anti-aircraft guns are probably the largest weapons that any guerrillas will ever use. The term 'anti-aircraft gun' has been used, but it should be remembered that such weapons can also have a tactical use against ground targets.

With the predominance of the surface-to-air air defence missile in many modern armed forces, the anti-aircraft gun has somewhat faded from use, but it is still an important defence weapon against fast low-flying aircraft, having a much faster response time than any missile and a capability of high fire rates, to improve the chances of obtaining a hit.

Guerrillas use anti-aircraft guns to defend their home bases, supply dumps and supply routes. Only the largest and most organized guerrilla groups are likely to have such weapons, a typical example being the Vietcong during the Vietnam conflict. The sheer bulk, lack of mobility and weight of even the smaller anti-aircraft guns prevents them from being used in any normal guerrilla combat, although during the later insurrection stages of a guerrilla campaign, heavy weapons such as anti-aircraft guns can be invaluable. They can also be used against security force installations, such as airfields and supply bases, but any rapid guerrilla withdrawal will almost certainly result in heavy weapons being left behind, the anti-aircraft guns among them.

One important anti-aircraft defence weapon in guerrilla use is the 0.50 (12.7 mm) Browning heavy machine gun. Slightly larger in calibre than the Browning is the series of 14.5 mm Soviet air defence weapons known as the ZPU. These are really heavy machine-guns that can be mounted in vehicles, but the most that guerrillas are likely to use are the series of towed weapons known as either the ZPU-1, ZPU-2 or ZPU-4, with the numeral indicating the number of guns carried. Even the lightest of these weapons, the ZPU-1, weighs 413 kg but it has an effective range against aircraft targets of 1,400 metres and has a cyclic rate of fire of 600 rpm.

ZPU guns are used by many countries, and guerrillas have found them to be very effective weapons. They were certainly used by guerrillas during the later stages of the Rhodesian war, and many other African guerrillas seem to have them - Unita and Polisario certainly have. PLO bases in the Middle East use ZPUs for base and perimeter defence (and for firing-off to impress visitors) and, as always, some have passed into Afghan Mujahadeen employment.

There is only one other anti-aircraft gun in guerrilla use, and that is another Soviet weapon, the 23 mm ZU-23. This may have one or two barrels, but most have two. Again, this is a weapon likely to be used only by the largest and best-organized guerrilla groups, for it is large and heavy, so heavy that it has to be towed around on a two-wheeled carriage. The ZU-23 weighs 950 kg and has a cyclic rate of fire from each barrel of up to 1,000 r.p.m. The effective range against air targets is 2,500 metres.

The main guerrilla users of this weapon are the PLO. They have been seen on newsreels firing away at Israeli aircraft flying at high altitudes over PLO bases (another example of the Beirut syndrome), and many were captured by the Israelis after their 1982 invasion of Lebanon. In an attempt to provide their ZU-23s with some measure of mobility the PLO mounted a few on the backs of civilian trucks, which made it all the easier for the Israelis to take them home as trophies.

Artillery

For the guerrilla, artillery means recoilless guns. Anything else is quite simply too heavy and immobile for guerrilla warfare.

The recoilless gun was originally developed before and during the Second World War for use by airborne forces, which had to travel and fight lightly-laden. So do guerrillas, so recoilless guns are almost tailor-made for guerrilla activities. Recoilless guns are relatively light, can fire large projectiles and are simple to operate, since all firing is likely to be carried out using direct fire and open sights.

The Chinese 14.5 mm Type 56 is a copy of the Soviet ZPU-4 and has been used by several guerrilla organizations, including the PLO and the Afghan Mujahadeen (T. Gander).

Recoilless guns do have disadvantages, however. The main one is that as they fire, the mass of propellant gas directed backwards to counterbalance the recoil forces kicks up a huge cloud of dust and debris, giving away the firing position. As with rocket exhaust, the recoilless gun exhaust is extremely dangerous to anyone who might get caught in its path for a considerable distance to the rear. Another disadvantage is that the ammunition is bulky. The recoilless gun has to use proportionally more propellant than a conventional gun, so even a relatively small recoilless gun round can be an awkward load to carry, adding to guerrilla supply problems.

Most recoilless guns in guerrilla use were designed to be anti-tank weapons. Thus although they have a long-range potential, their sighting systems are meant for direct fire only and are usually limited to 1,500 metres or so on the larger calibres ~ smaller calibres achieve less. On some models, only anti-armour warheads are available, but since such warheads are equally useful against many other types of target, this matters little.

The recoilless gun is now little used outside countries that have received Soviet military aid. Although many countries continue to use the American 106 mm M27 'recoilless rifle', this weapon is seldom seen in guerrilla hands. Instead, the smaller American 57 mm M18 'recoilless rifle' is retained. This gun is fired with a monopod as a fire support and weighs only 22 kg. It was designed during the late stages of the Second World War to be an anti-armour weapon with an effective maximum range of 450 metres – its maximum range is 4,000 metres. In its day, it was a remarkable weapon, but it is now regarded as obsolete.

But to guerrillas the M18 is a very useful gun. It can be used to attack blockhouses, knock down buildings and attack light armoured vehicles. It can be carried in and out of action by only two men (one at a pinch) yet is reasonably accurate and hard-hitting. It can be found in guerrilla use in many places throughout South-East Asia and South America (the Peruvian 'Shining Path' guerrillas have used them to force their way into bank strong-rooms). Until recently, the Chinese produced both the M18 (as the Type 36) and its ammunition. Several countries in South America did the same.

The Soviet equivalent of the M18 is the 82 mm B-10. Although long out of service with the Warsaw Pact nations, the B-10 is still used in several Middle and Far Eastern countries; as always, the Chinese produced a copy, the Type 65. The B-10 is a larger and heavier design than the M18, weighing 88 kg when being towed. It can be hand-towed by the muzzle, a common practice with light recoilless guns, with the tripod carriage folded up under the barrel. The single-axle carriage is removed for firing. As the B-10 was designed to be a multi-purpose gun, it can fire 4.5 kg high-explosive projectiles to a range of 4,500 metres.

Among the main users of the B-10 again, are, the Mujahadeen. They have used their B-10s against forts occupied by the Afghan and Soviet security forces, to variable effect, and B-10s have also been employed against Soviet supply convoys. B-10s have also been encountered in the Middle East, and the gun was owned by the Vietcong at one time.

Another recoilless gun used by guerrillas is the Czech 82 mm T-21 Tarasnice. This gun has several attractive features for guerrilla consideration, not the least being the provision of a pair of wheels for towing. Although it is meant to be a shoulder-fired weapon, the T-21 weighs 20 kg complete, so a hand-towing facility is useful. The towing handle folds up next to the barrel in action. The weight of the projectile fired by the T-21 is 2.13 kg and the maximum range on the sights is 600 metres.

One Chinese recoilless gun that is an Afghan guerrilla favourite is the 75 mm Type 56. This is easily recognized by its distinctive curved wheel support carriage and wide-spoked wheels. The Type 56 is fired from its wheels and has a maximum range of 6,675 metres. The barrel of the Type 56 was copied from the American 75 mm M20 recoilless gun, a weapon long since withdrawn from use by any Western forces. The Type 56 is another weapon used by the Mujahadeen, and it was also used by the Vietcong. A similar weapon, the 75 mm Type 52, uses the same gun barrel mounted on a tripod carriage on which the towing wheels are raised for firing.

There are other models of recoilless gun, but the examples mentioned above cover the main types likely to be encountered in guerrilla service.

INDEX